# 100 YEARS PORTSTEWART

## The Story of a Keswick Convention

Bill + Leta
God Bless Joe
19/7/13

## Joseph Fell

# Commendations:

*The grateful celebration of anniversaries has rich biblical precedent and we are indebted to Dr Fell for his careful research into the first hundred years of the Convention. Set firmly in its variable political and social context, this is not simply a centenary account of past meetings. It is the story of specific personalities directly involved in the formation, development and continuance of 'Portstewart' and, more importantly, of lives changed by its dynamic, ever-relevant message.*
**The Rev. Dr Raymond Brown, former Principal of Spurgeon's College, London and an internationally known Keswick Speaker.**

*The Portstewart Convention has an important place in the wider Keswick movement, not least because of the strength of evangelicalism in Northern Ireland. Joseph Fell has produced a detailed and fascinating account of this Convention, and all those interested in the Keswick story will find what he has written valuable.*
**The Rev. Dr Ian M. Randall, Senior Research Fellow, Spurgeon's College, London, and International Baptist Theological Seminary, Prague.**

*I thoroughly enjoyed reading the marvellous account of the North of Ireland Keswick Convention by Reverend Dr Joseph Fell, a Presbyterian Minister and an acknowledged authority on Keswick. He has given sterling service to the Convention since his early days, as well as serving as Secretary (1991-2004) and a renewal Chairman since 2004. We wish him well this year at the Centenary celebrations. I know this book will bring spiritual satisfaction to all who read it. The Convention has invited dedicated men of God who brought the Bible alive to the congregations. But we need to read prayerfully the last two chapters. Both challenge the present generation to respond anew to the fundamentals of the Christian Faith. It has been a privilege to know the author, admire his scholarship, and to be enriched by this book.*
**The Rev. Professor David Ben Rees, PhD, Liverpool, England.**

*Rev Joseph Fell proved to be an excellent researcher, well equipped in terms of knowledge, perspective, experience and motivation. He has shown his ability with this publication to make an important and valuable contribution for the Centenary of the North of Ireland Keswick Convention. The Keswick story in Ireland was largely untold, and the author succeeded in telling the exciting history of a movement that has inspired countless Christian people to dedicate themselves to God in the power of the Holy Spirit in all spheres of life. It was my privilege to be one of the promoters of Rev. Joseph Fell who submitted his dissertation on this topic for a PhD under the supervision of Greenwich School of Theology (UK) and the North-West University in South Africa.* **Prof. A. le R. du Plooy ThD, Dean of the Faculty of Theology.**

*The Rev. Dr Joseph Fell has written a new book about the Portstewart Convention, to be launched later this year at the Convention's Centenary. He has titled it "One hundred years at Portstewart". In that period many believers in the Tent were confronted by their sins and failures, and then in response to the teaching, by repentance, faith and surrender to Jesus, they were empowered by the Spirit for attractive living and effective service. I remember reading about a preacher in a previous generation who loved the narrative about Pentecost, and every time he read it, as he closed the Bible slowly he prayed, "and Lord, please do it again."* **The Very Rev. Dr W.M. Craig, Convention Chairman 1976 – 1991**

*The Portstewart Convention was born on the very verge of World War I. Long after that War's end, for a hundred years, it has continued another - against the world around us, the flesh within us, and the devil beyond us. It has served as a beacon of hope for those battle-weary souls needing reassurance of Christ's victory in the past through His Cross, in the present through His Spirit, and in the future through His glorious return. Be informed, engaged, encouraged and illuminated as Joseph Fell whistle stops us through a century of the Convention's history, with its heroes and saints, great and small.* **The Rev. Dr. Steve Brady, Principal, Moorlands College & Trustee, The Keswick Convention**

# Contents

# Acknowledgements

The Ministry of God's Word at the North of Ireland Keswick Convention has moulded my life ever since I began to attend in 1959. My own Minister, the Rev. Dr Thomas Fitch of Ravenhill Presbyterian Church, Belfast was a Keswick man and his ministry strongly reflected Keswick spirituality. For many years he took a party from the Congregation to Keswick. In 1965, as a University student, I joined the party and had the privilege of being present at the significant morning Bible Readings given by the late Rev Dr J.R.W. Stott which were subsequently published by Inter Varsity Press under the title *Men Made New*. That same year, I heard Dr Stott expound John 10 at the Convention Ministers' Meeting and that was a formative experience for me.

The Rev. Ernest Kevan, Principal of London Bible College, on his first visit to Keswick as a Speaker, delivered the Bible Readings in 1953 and they were subsequently published by Pickering and Inglis under the title *The Saving Work of the Holy Spirit*. He was an interesting choice! The previous year the Rev. Graham Scroggie had given Bible Readings from Romans in which he had clearly expounded the usual understanding of Keswick teaching at that time. However, Kevan offered a more Reformed interpretation. Keswick was changing and in 1965 Dr Stott's Bible Readings were a significant watershed. His masterful exposition of Romans 5-8 was both illuminating and inspiring. I remember something of the debate that the Bible Readings caused.

I have been a member of the North of Ireland Keswick Committee since 1986, serving as Secretary from 1991 until 2004 when I was appointed Chairman. I want to express my thanks to several people. Mr J. Lawson McDonald, a former Secretary and my immediate predecessor as Chairman of the Convention, for his help in providing some primary source material. The Very Rev. Dr W.M. Craig, a former Convention Chairman, gave me great encouragement, insights and many personal memories. The Rev. Dr Raymond Brown, former Principal of Spurgeon's College London and an acknowledged Keswick expert, kindly read my script and offered me helpful advice. Mr Donald Garvie of the Union Theological College, Belfast was always generous in providing material for my studies.

While attending the North of Ireland Keswick in 1968, I met a young nurse who would become my wife. Her name was Sheila Dunlop and her father, the Very Rev. Dr James Dunlop, was the Convention Chairman at that time. Sheila has given me her full support as my involvement in the Convention's work deepened. Throughout my years as Chairman she has acted as hostess at the House Party. I want to thank her for her patience, understanding and encouragement, as in our retirement from active Congregational ministry she encouraged and supported me in my academic research into the Convention which has meant so much to us, both before and throughout our married life.

# Introduction

Y ou are about to read an exciting story.

This book is not intended to be a dry historical account of a Christian event held each year at Portstewart. It is the story of a Movement that has inspired countless Christian people to live to serve God in the power of the Holy Spirit at home, in their local church and to the ends of the earth.

'The North of Ireland Keswick Convention' has been held continuously at Portstewart, Co. Londonderry, N. Ireland since 1914. It is probably true however, that many of the people, who enter the Convention's large marquee located at the corner of Enfield Street and Convention Avenue in the seaside resort, are unaware of the history of the event, held there for one week in the Summer ever since. In fact, the Avenue takes its name from the Convention, known later and for many decades as 'The Portstewart Convention'. In 2005 'Keswick at Portstewart' was adopted as its working name.

Two other books have been written to tell the Convention's story. The first in 1934, by the Rev. Canon Oswald W. Scott, the Rector of St Paul's Church of Ireland in York Street, Belfast was entitled, *The Story of the Portstewart Convention*. The other, in 1988, by the Very Rev. Dr John T. Carson, Minister of Trinity Presbyterian Church, Bangor, Co. Down and former Moderator of the Presbyterian Church in Ireland was entitled, *The River of God is Full*. A shorter booklet also by Dr Carson, *Ocean Fulness*, was published in 1963 and contained a flavour of Keswick Ministry from some of its well-known Speakers.

It is acknowledged that the Keswick story in Ireland is largely untold. A few minor references in books authorized by the Keswick Convention Council in Cumbria, England and in a number of biographies, autobiographies and histories highlight both the place and the role of 'The Portstewart Convention'. In fact, there were other Keswicks and Keswick style Conventions held in Ireland from as early as 1876. This book will give a succinct account of a number of them.

The story of the North of Ireland Keswick Convention is one of remarkable vision, adventuresome faith and dedication. While the founders of the Convention were busy making their plans, the local Newspapers highlighted the political fears of the populace and the calls for a Provisional Government in Ulster. The Convention's founders were convinced that the Keswick Message of full salvation in Christ had a vital role to play in the life of the Church and in society.

The joint founders of the Convention were the Rev. Canon Oswald W. Scott, then Rector of Gilford, Co. Down, and Mr R.H. Stephens Richardson, an evangelical Quaker. They both brought unique skills to the Convention and gathered a formidable team around them, to ensure the Convention would not only develop, but that it would also survive to celebrate its Centenary in 2013.

Like any other organisation, the Convention has passed through some very difficult times. Its leaders have sought to guide it through much troubled water as this book will show. Over 100 years it is certain that errors of judgment have been made. If that is the case, it is equally certain that they were made by Godly leaders who sought the Glory of God, the good of the Convention and its attendees.

It is clear, even from a quick perusal of the Northern Ireland scene in 2013, that the Convention does not hold the position it once occupied when thousands attended the meetings every day in the 2,500 seater marquee, and when the Committee sponsored local Conventions in many centres throughout the country. *The Daily Express* of 20th June, 1938, described the Portstewart Convention as "Ulster's most powerful spiritual force".

In 2013 however, the Convention is more confident about its place and role, both in the rapidly changing ecclesiastical scene and among other large Christian gatherings in N. Ireland. It has often been said that a Conference has a subject while a Convention has an object. The object of 'Keswick at Portstewart' is the glory of God through the proclamation of His Word, directed particularly to the consecration of the attendees to the Lord, the local church and His work in every place, in the power of the Holy Spirit.

It is impossible to cover every facet of the Convention in this short book. The author takes full responsibility for its contents and apologies to any people who feel that they have been ignored or misrepresented.

*Joseph Fell*

May, 2013

# Chapter 1

# The Convention is conceived in 1913

I n 1914, the Keswick Convention Movement was an international phenomenon and Keswick's distinctive spirituality was well-known throughout the evangelical community in Ireland. Founded in 1875, the parent Keswick Convention drew large crowds to the picturesque town in the English Lake District from which it received its name.

Our story begins however, in the Rectory of St. Paul's Church of Ireland Parish in Gilford, Co. Down when the Rev. Oswald W. Scott, decided to attend the 1913 Keswick Convention. His first visit had been in 1893 and at every subsequent visit his ministry had been enriched. The 1913 Keswick Convention changed his life significantly, and he believed that God was urging him to establish a Keswick Convention in the North of Ireland. The Speakers at Keswick in 1913 were:

| | |
|---|---|
| Rev. Hubert Brooke | Rev. Canon R.C. Joynt |
| Mr James D. Crosbie | Rev. Harrington C. Lees |
| Rev. W.Y. Fullerton | Rev. W. Graham Scroggie |
| Rev. George C. Grubb | Rt Rev. Bishop Taylor Smith |
| Rev. E.H. Hopkins | Rev. Prebendary H.W. Webb-Peploe |
| Rev. Charles Inwood | Rev. F.S. Webster |

When the Rev. Scott returned to Gilford, the desire remained unabated and after prayer he decided to share it with a Quaker friend, Mr R.H. Stephens Richardson of Moyallan near Portadown. The Rev. Scott was glad to learn that God had laid a similar desire upon the heart and mind of Mr Richardson. This formidable and Godly friendship was to set in motion a sequence of events which was to bring untold blessings to many people. In many ways the unfolding story of the Convention is the product of their faith, prayer and work. God had brought them together in His Sovereignty. They lived in the same geographical area and shared a common longing that God would bless the country at that critical time.

Interestingly in 1875, when the Rev. Canon Harford-Battersby was moved by God to call meetings for the 'Promotion of Scriptural Holiness' at Keswick, he made contact with Mr Robert Wilson, a Quaker from Cockermouth. The Keswick Convention and the North of Ireland Keswick Convention were both founded by men with evangelical Anglican and Quaker convictions.

Scott and Richardson, not only shared the vision for a North of Ireland Keswick Convention, but they had the ability and faith to see it realised. Both men sounded out the support for their shared vision from a number of influential friends and colleagues. The services of two leading Belfast evangelicals; the Rev. James Hunter of Knock Presbyterian Church and the Very Rev. Dr Henry Montgomery of the Shankill Road Mission were utilised. Hunter wrote a letter to some Presbyterian colleagues:

> September 3rd
>
> Dear
>
> A few friends who are interested in the Keswick Convention Movement have had it laid upon their hearts to get up a Convention on similiar lines in the North of Ireland, if it be the Lord's will; and in order that the matter may be carefully and prayerfully considered, they are venturing to summon a Meeting of those who are in sympathy with Keswick, for Thursday, the 11th September, at 11:30am, in the Minor Hall of the YMCA, Belfast.
>
> It is hoped that this Meeting will be addressed by Mr J.D. Crosbie DL, the Chairman of the Killarney Convention, and one of the Trustees of the Keswick Council, and the Rev. Chas. Inwood, one of the Keswick Speakers.
>
> Yours sincerely,
>
> J. Hunter.

At the meeting on 11th September, 1913, Mr J.D. Crosbie DL of Ballyheigue Castle, Co. Kerry and Rev. Charles Inwood, former Minister of Knock

Methodist Church, Belfast, spoke persuasively about the Keswick Convention and its Biblical emphasis. Those who attended decided to proceed with a Convention and the following were elected as the planning Committee:

> Very Rev. Dean Dowse, Archdeacon Spence, Very Rev. Dr Montgomery, Rev. J. Hunter, Rev. W. W. Pyper, Rev. J.T. Wilson, Rev. Alex Egan, Rev. T. Rogers, Rev. Canon Moore, Rev. S. Simms. Canon Cooke, Rev. Dr Stephenson, Rev. R. Ussher Greer, Rev. L.P. Story, Rev. W.J. Hanson, Rev. Hedley Brownrigg, Rev. Alex McCrea, Rev. Oswald Scott, Rev. John Ross, Rev. W. Witherow, Mr W.H. McLaughlin DL, Mr Arthur Pim, Mr H. Stephens Richardson, Mr Joseph McCurry, Mr J.T. Ward, Mr Samuel A. Robinson, Mr R.L. McKeown, Mr A. Crawford Brown, Mr William Fulton, Mr J.W. Storey, Mr Samuel G. Montgomery.

True to Keswick's ecumenicity, of those elected four were Anglican Clergymen, (Cooke, Stephenson, Scott, and Warren); eight were Presbyterian Ministers, (Montgomery, Hunter, Ross, Little, Rogers, Simms, Witherow and Smyth); two were Quakers, (Richardson and Pim); one was a Congregational Minister, (Hanson); two were Bankers, (McCurry and Robinson); one was a Lawyer (Fulton); and the others included, Mr R.L. McKeown (Presbyterian) the Secretary of the Qua Iboe Mission. From the beginning of the life of the North of Ireland Keswick Convention the largest influence was Presbyterian and Reformed, reflecting the proportionate spread of the local Protestant denominations. The Rev. Scott and Mr Richardson were appointed as Joint Honorary Secretaries and Mr Joseph McCurry was appointed as Treasurer. At the next Committee Meeting held on January 13th 1914, the Very Rev. Dr H. Montgomery was elected Chairman of the Committee.

Henry Montgomery wrote to *The Belfast News Letter* the next day, "we could not be ignorant of the heavy cloud overhanging Ireland and that was a strong reason for holding a Convention". The critical national and international situation did not deter the leaders, but rather it inspired them to bring God's Word to address it.

Chapter 2

# The Convention is born in 1914

Having decided to proceed with the formation of the Convention, two other very important decisions had to be made. Where would it meet and when? Keswick style Conventions for the deepening of Spiritual Life had been held in Dublin, Cork, Killarney, Mulranney, Belfast, Bangor, Lisburn, Fivemiletown and elsewhere throughout Ireland before 1914.

In 1902, the Keswick Convention sponsored a 'Prayer Circle' ministry for worldwide Revival. *The Life of Faith*, edited by the Rev. Evan Hopkins an early Keswick theologian, was the semi-official magazine of Keswick and it carried reports of the Circles and their numerous locations throughout the United Kingdom. As early as 1903, the Rev. H. Montgomery had written in *The Life of Faith*, that people were, "... really praying that God shall pour out His Spirit on all flesh for it is His will that the Gospel shall be preached as a witness to all nations". In Ireland there were numerous Prayer Circles and there can be no doubt that they encouraged the extension of the Keswick Movement.

Various locations were discussed by the Committee including Rostrevor and Portrush where Prayer Circles were in existence. Although there was no Prayer Circle in Portstewart the Committee decided on 13th January, 1914, that the Convention should be located there. On 13th February, Dr Montgomery and Mr Richardson visited Portstewart and were greatly encouraged by the response and welcome given by the Rev. David Aiken of the local Presbyterian Church and the Rev. E.R. Moncrieff of Agherton Church of Ireland Parish Church. Two local Secretaries were appointed at Portstewart, namely Miss Moncrieff and Miss Anderson and, with Mr Henry they made enquiries about Guest Houses, local halls for Meetings, a suitable house for the Speakers and other practical arrangements.

At the Committee Meeting on 13th January, 1914, the official name of the Convention was adopted; 'The North of Ireland Keswick Convention'. However from 1917 it was known commonly as 'The Portstewart Convention'. The dates for the first Convention were set as Monday 22nd June – Friday 27th June, 1914 and Mr J. D. Crosbie and the Rev. Charles Inwood used their good Keswick connections to secure the Speakers. On the 23rd May, 1914, *The Belfast News Letter* carried the following preliminary announcement:

### The North of Ireland Keswick Convention
### for the Deepening of Spiritual Life.
will be held (D.V.) in Portstewart
Monday 22nd June – Saturday 27th June 1914.
Chairman
James D. Crosbie Esq., DL
Ballyheigue Castle, Co. Kerry.
Speakers:
Rev. Hubert Brooke MA
Rev. Evan H. Hopkins (London)
Rev. Charles Inwood FRCS
Rev. J. Chalmers Lyons (Harrogate)
Rev. Dr Alexander Smellie.
Chairman of Committee:
Rev. Henry Montgomery MA, DD
Honorary Secretaries:
Rev. Oswald W. Scott MA
The Vicarage, Gilford
Mr H. Stephens Richardson
Drumlyn, Moyallon

The first suggested daily programme for the Convention in 1914 was:

Prayer Meeting at 7:30am
Bible Reading  10:00am
Convention Meeting 11:30am-12:45pm
Afternoon Meeting on certain days at 3:30pm
Evening Meeting at 6:30pm

On 28th April, 1914 the programme was further refined:

Convention Meeting 11:45am instead of 11:30am
Afternoon Meetings – Wednesday
and Missionary Thursday at 3:30pm.
Evening Meeting at 7:00pm instead of 6:30pm

Not knowing how many people would attend, the Committee hired a tent and arranged to provide bench type seating to accommodate 500 people. *The Belfast News Letter* of 23rd June, 1914, commented: "The Conference is to be held in a spacious and comfortable tent, convenient to the handsome Presbyterian Church and on an eminence overlooking the beautiful bay and strand". A bookstall was organised by Miss Woods of Portrush at which people could purchase the Keswick Hymnbook at a discount of 25 per cent and other suitable literature. Mr Pim, a Quaker, provided the Keswick Motto, 'All One in Christ Jesus'. Interestingly it was another Quaker, already mentioned in our story, Mr Robert Wilson who suggested that Keswick take that text from Galatians 3:28 as their Motto. It has remained the Keswick Motto ever since!

The Committee were busy publicizing the Convention using 16 local and national newspapers including the Dublin based *Irish Times*. Clearly the leadership wanted to appeal to the whole island. In addition, contact was made with the Midland Railway Company about special trains running at a convenient timetable and at reduced fares.

*The Christian* on July 2nd 1914, carried a full report of the Convention. The first Scripture to be expounded was by the Chairman, Mr J.D. Crosbie from Psalm 50:5, "Gather My saints together unto Me; those who have made a covenant by sacrifice". The Rev. Charles Inwood preached at the opening meeting from Joshua 3:5, "Sanctify yourselves, for tomorrow the Lord will do wonders among you". *The Christian* reported, "The next day found a still larger number gathered". At the Prayer Meeting that day the Rev. Evan Hopkins brought a message from Hosea 14. The morning Bible Readings by the Rev. Dr Alexander Smellie took as their subject, 'The Holy Spirit'. In his first address the Rev. J. Chalmers Lyons used Luke 19:10 as his text, "pointing out that the deeper teaching of Christianity must be preceded by entrance upon the Christian life".

The Missionary Meeting was addressed by the Rev. Hubert Brooke who gave "a most inspiring and illuminating exposition of the opening verses of the Book of Ezra". Three Missionaries reported at the Meeting. They were

"Rev. J. Omelvena of the Irish Presbyterian Church, Mrs Bill of the Qua Iboe Mission; and Mr George Swan of the Egypt General Mission". These three Missions were to figure regularly at the subsequent Convention Missionary Meetings. The offering, which was distributed among them, amounted to £25, 6 shillings and 4 pence. Interestingly, and according to the Bank of England Inflation Calculator, that amount would have been worth a remarkable £2,366 in 2011.

On 25th June, 1914, *The Belfast News Letter* under the headline, 'Keswick Convention at Portstewart' asserted:

> Interest in their meetings in the North of Ireland is beyond all expectations and the large marquee is scarcely able to accommodate all who seek admission. All the seats from various halls in Portstewart were put at the disposal of the Committee.

*The Christian* reported, "The closing day found the tide of blessing still rising" and that the organisers "most sanguine expectations have been exceeded". *The Christian* also reported that the closing night attracted 800 people so that the marquee "was crowded to its utmost capacity".

The Leaders of the Convention followed the Keswick principle of working with the local Churches. They wanted leaders of major Denominations to be present at the opening Meeting in June, 1914. Their aim was to be true to Keswick's Motto, "All One in Christ Jesus". Greetings were received from the Rev. Samuel T. Boyd, Vice President of the Methodist Church in Ireland who could not be present due to duties at the Methodist Conference and from the Very Rev. Dr Macauley, of Portadown, the former Moderator of the General Assembly of the Presbyterian Church in Ireland, who commented that, "the great need of our Northern Province is just that which the Convention aims at being the means of promoting – a revival of vital Godliness in the heart and lives of members of our Churches". In addition the Rev. O. W. Scott read a letter from the Rt Rev. Charles D'Arcy, the Bishop of the local Church of Ireland Diocese. *The Belfast News Letter,* of 23rd June, 1914 reported it:

> Will you kindly convey to the Convention my hearty welcome to the Diocese and say that I hope very sincerely that the gatherings may prove helpful spiritually to those who take part in them? It is a time when united action on the part of Christian people of various Churches should be especially valuable. I trust that you all may be blessed.

The first Convention met amid perilous times in the North of Ireland. The Home Rule debate was still raging, the Ulster Covenant had been signed and the Ulster Volunteer Force had been formed. The Home Rule emergency had taken the form of a religious crusade. *The Belfast News Letter* announced "A Time of Prayer for the Present Crisis", to be held on Monday 22nd June, the very day the Convention started. During the first Convention the Amending Bill was presented to Parliament. This allowed any of the six Ulster Counties to vote itself out of Home Rule for six years. In addition, the question of universal suffrage was hitting the headlines in the UK press and *The Northern Whig* of 23rd June, 1914 reported that militant suffragettes and their supporters would be shadowed by the police. The day after the first Convention ended, Archduke Franz Ferdinand and his wife were assassinated in Sarajevo and the First World War was to begin exactly one month later.

The North of Ireland in 1914, was divided politically and was prosperous industrially. Collins, comments that "Belfast was in its heyday at the turn of the century". Shipbuilding, rope making, tobacco manufacturing and linen production were booming. James Larkin, the founder of the Irish Transport and General Workers Union, Christian Socialist and Temperance Campaigner led the 1907 Strike in an epic struggle between master and worker. Suspicion in the work place between Roman Catholics and Protestants was never far from the surface and often exploded into militant expulsions.

The Convention offered hope in a very difficult and dangerous time. It was something new. Many believing people had longings for Revival as they remembered the 1859 Ulster and the Welsh Revivals of the early 20th century. Respected and well-known leaders were involved. Dr Montgomery for example, was described as "one of the most beloved Ministers in Belfast" and the other Committee members were a virtual 'Who's Who' of the local evangelical and business scene.

# Chapter 3

# The English Connection

T he North of Ireland Keswick Convention "for the deepening of spiritual life and the promotion of practical holiness" had its immediate roots in Great Britain. To set the scene it is necessary to go back into the eighteenth and nineteenth centuries to examine briefly the contemporary teaching about holiness.

The Rev. John Wesley (1703-1791) exercised a powerful ministry throughout the British Isles and overseas. This led. in due course, to the founding of the Methodist Church. He was an extensive reader and a capable theologian. Wesley regarded practical holiness as the major consequence for anyone justified by grace through faith in Christ. He believed that 'Salvation' was not only "deliverance from hell, or going to heaven; but a present deliverance from sin, a restoration of the soul to its primitive health, its original purity, a recovery of the divine nature, the renewal of our souls after the image of God in righteousness and true holiness, in justice, mercy and truth". 'Sanctification', according to Wesley, is a process derived from a definite experience of a second work of grace, expressed as 'perfect love', in which the individual becomes devoid of self-interest. He believed that sin was not destroyed in the believer, but that it was suspended in the life of the sanctified person, and thus they are enabled to live above all known sin, with good works becoming the inevitable consequence. The remedy for humanity's systemic sinfulness is entire sanctification, a personal, definitive work of God's grace by which the war within oneself might cease and the heart be fully released from rebellion into wholehearted love for God and others. Wesleyan theology is decidedly ethical.

This view of sanctification differs from the Presbyterian and Reformed interpretation which teaches that sanctification is both definitive and progressive. The believer is declared righteous by justification and then, by God's grace, is "enabled more and more to die unto sin and live unto righteousness". The Christian is at once a 'sinner' and a 'saint'. The person justified by grace through faith is saved for time and for eternity, but there is a struggle as he or she lives for God's glory and accepts the personal responsibility to advance their sanctification.

The spiritual core of the nineteenth Century was the 1859 Evangelical Awakening which, under God, changed the face of many parts of Great Britain and Ulster. The century was also characterized by a remarkable amount of evangelical activism. Among the well-known evangelical philanthropists were the 7th Earl of Shaftesbury (1801-1885) and Dr Thomas Barnado (1845-1905) who, fired by their Gospel beliefs, did much to help alleviate the conditions of the poor and effect change through Parliamentary legislation. Historian, David Edwards comments that Barnardo, "before his death in 1905 had assumed responsibility for the rebuilding of almost 60,000 young lives". In addition, Professor David Bebbington has highlighted the rise of Romanticism through the writings of Coleridge and its infiltration into evangelicalism in the century.

In the last quarter of the century, however, the Church in Great Britain was under pressure from various quarters; ecclesiastically through the Oxford Movement, theologically through German Rationalism and Higher Criticism, scientifically through the writings of Charles Darwin, socially through the writing of Karl Marx and philosophically through 'Monism'. The popular book *Self Help,* by Samuel Smiles, extolled the virtues of self-advancement. All these challenged the Church at various levels. Controversy was in the air and the relationship between the Established Church and the Nonconformists was frigid. Many professing Christians followed an introspective brand of Christianity that soon developed into gloom, joylessness and a lack of confidence in the Bible. The Church was being drained of its joy. Meanwhile in 1873-74, D.L. Moody and Ira D. Sankey conducted evangelistic campaigns in the largest cities in England, Scotland and Ireland. These were unprecedented in magnitude and far reaching in their influence. Many tens of thousands were swept into the Kingdom of Christ and Christians throughout the land had their spiritual lives quickened and interest in overseas mission received a new impulse.

Into this situation came a holiness movement from the United States, promoted in Britain chiefly by Mr and Mrs Robert Pearsall Smith in 1873. They came from a Methodist / Quaker background and had been influenced by people such as, Phoebe Palmer (1807-1874) who according to *The Oxford Dictionary of the Christian Church* was,

> a Methodist lay leader, who taught that perfection in love was a second blessing distinct from regeneration and that it eliminated all sinful desires. It spread initially through meetings in private houses, and was fostered by the journal, *Guide to Christian Perfection* (1839 – 45) which became the *Guide to Holiness* (1846 – 1901).

Palmer found in her experience that "one act of faith was not sufficient to ensure a continuance in 'the way of holiness' but that a continuous act of faith was requisite". Sanctification, she taught, was to be claimed by the individual immediately and she based her emphasis on 2nd Corinthians 6:2, "Now is the accepted time, now is the day of salvation". This is not the common interpretation of the text, but it was the verse she used. Palmer talked about "entire salvation" and from her Wesleyan background she preached about it as "perfection in holiness" or "perfection in love".

In an attempt to evaluate the Holiness teaching emerging in Britain, sixteen people met in the Curzon Chapel, London on 1st May, 1873. Among them were the Revs Evan H. Hopkins and E.W. Moore who were to become significant leaders of the future Keswick Convention. E.W. Moore wrote about the experience:

> I was pressed to go and hear an address on this subject. I had disliked some of the papers in *The Christian*, and laid it aside and refused to take it in. However, I went, expecting to hear some new doctrine. The speaker said great blessing had come into his life through deep searchings of heart, and unreserved surrender and trust in Jesus. I said "Search me O God". He showed me things I had never seen before and I yielded them and myself to Him. .. the Lord Jesus had come and taken the throne of my heart.

Subsequently, a two day Conference, held at Mildmay on 20th and 21st January, 1874, for the promotion of spiritual life, was called by the Rev. William Pennefather (1816-1873). He had convened these annual gatherings for Church workers, firstly at Barnet from 1856, then at Mildmay from 1864 and "personal holiness" was a recurring subject. At the 1874 Mildmay Conference, the Rev. W.E. Boardman, Henry Varley and Henry Grattan Guinness were the prominent speakers and *The Christian's Pathway to Power* records that, "God was at work" during the Conference and that "the fulness of the Gospel had been opened up to them". Mildmay gave the Holiness Movement in Britain its final major impetus towards the Broadlands Conference which led to the Keswick Convention in 1875, to the Dublin Convention in 1876 and ultimately to the North of Ireland Keswick at Portstewart in 1914.

Through the magazine *The Christian's Pathway to Power,* first published in Britain in February 1874, the Smiths promoted their concept of holiness and the victorious Christian life.

> We believe the Word of God teaches that the normal Christian life is one of uniform sustained victory over known sin; and that no temptation is permitted to happen to us without a way of escape being provided by God, so that we may be able to bear it. ... His Promises are as great as His Commands.

Robert Pearsall Smith's book *Holiness through Faith* (1870) and Mrs Hannah Whitall Smith's, *The Christian Secret of a Happy Life* (1874) influenced many people. The Smiths, in turn, had been influenced by the writings of Presbyterian Minister the Rev. W.E. Boardman, author in 1859 of *The Higher Christian Life*. In his book Boardman gives examples of people such as Martin Luther (1483 – 1546), Jonathan Edwards (1703 - 1758), William Carvosso (1750 – 1835) and Merle D'Aubigne (1794 – 1872) as men who received a second experience of Christ; and as their Christian life began with justification by faith so they discovered subsequently, that sanctification was also by faith. *The Christian* of 9th January, 1868 reported Mr Smith as teaching that the secret of holiness lay, "simply in ceasing from all efforts of your own, and trusting Jesus". Elsewhere Mrs Smith asserts that, "in order for a lump of clay to be made into a beautiful vessel; it must be entirely abandoned to the potter, and must lie passive in his hands". Mr and Mrs Smith and their life and ministry in America, Great Britain and Europe is well documented by Nigel Scotland in his book *Apostles of the Spirit and Fire* (2009). Another and previous contributor to the American Holiness Movement was Dr Asa Mahan, the President of Oberlin College. His book *Scriptural Doctrine of Christian Perfection* (1839) was widely read.

In the April, 1874 edition of *The Christian's Pathway to Power,* Pearsall Smith offered three steps to the Higher Christian Life:

1. Convince yourself that it is according to Scripture.
2. Be sure that you are willing to enter into it and live the life it necessitates.
3. Claim it as your present possession in Christ Jesus or, to say it in 3 words, your needs are Knowledge, Consecration, and Faith.

Three major Conferences were held at which the Smiths, the Revs Dr Asa Mahan, W.E. Boardman, Evan Hopkins etc. participated. The first was held at Broadlands in Hampshire, the home of William Cowper-Temple, from July 17th–23rd, 1874. The second was held at Oxford, from August 29th-7th September 1874 and the third at Brighton, from 29th May-7th June 1875.

Broadlands had been the location of annual and multifarious conferences. The 1874 conference was attended by about 100 people and *The Christian's Pathway to Power* of August 1874 commented: "No description could ever convey the wonderful sense of the presence and power of God which attended these six days of waiting upon the Lord". Charles Harford records the main themes for this gathering:

The Scriptural possibilities of faith in the life of the Christian in the daily walk (a) as to maintained communion with God; and (b) as to victory over all known sin.

These were the topics that were kept prayerfully and steadily in mind during these days of waiting upon God.

... Such was the absorbing interest felt by all that no difficulty was found in gathering guests at seven o'clock in the cool of the morning: and it was an effort to separate when the breakfast hour of nine came. At ten o'clock conversational meetings were held ... Meetings for ladies only, were also arranged, and at three o'clock conversational meetings were held, followed by a general meeting at four o'clock. After tea Bible readings were given till the regular evening meeting.

Theodore Monod, a Parisian Pastor, wrote the well-known Keswick hymn "The Altered Ego" at Broadlands.

O the bitter shame and sorrow,
That a time could ever be,
When I let the Saviour's pity

Plead in vain, and proudly answered,
"All of self, and none of Thee!"

Yet He found me; I beheld Him
Bleeding on th'accursèd tree,
Heard Him pray, "Forgive them, Father!"
And my wistful heart said faintly,
"Some of self, and some of Thee!"

Day by day His tender mercy,
Healing, helping, full and free,
Sweet and strong, and ah! so patient,
Brought me lower, while I whispered,
"Less of self, and more of Thee!"

Higher than the highest heavens,
Deeper than the deepest sea,
Lord, Thy love at last hath conquered:
Grant me now my supplication,
"None of self, and all of Thee!"

Harford quotes a letter from Monod:

> The difference between those Broadlands meetings and many
> others that I have attended is just the difference between a
> flower and the name of a flower. Christians too often meet only
> to talk about good and precious things: peace, joy, love, and so
> on, but there we actually had the very things themselves. I cannot
> be grateful enough to God for having led me into such a soul-
> satisfying and God-glorifying faith.

Again, Harford writes, "the account of the 1874 Broadlands Conference
was read far and wide, and awakened considerable interest. Many, who had
before attended meetings of the kind, were led to cry to God for the fulness
of the Spirit". It was at the close of the meetings at Broadlands that someone
remarked: "We must repeat these meetings on a larger scale, when all who
desire can attend. It was suggested by the late beloved Sir Arthur Blackwood,
who was present at Broadlands, that this proposed Convention should be
held at Oxford, during vacation time".

'The Oxford Union Meetings for the Promotion of Scriptural Holiness'
were convened in late August 1874. It had been agreed that Pearsall Smith
should write the letter of invitation. In the letter dated 8th August, 1874, he

explained that the event was to be focused on meeting with God. He wrote:

> In every part of Christendom the God of all grace has given many of His children a feeling of deep dissatisfaction with their present spiritual state, and a strong conviction that the truths they believe might and should exercise a power over their hearts and lives, altogether beyond anything they have as yet experienced.

Any theological differences between participants were to remain unmentioned. Monod's hymn was printed on the programme. Various types of helpful meetings were held. Mr R.P Smith, Mrs R.P. Smith, Dr A. Mahan etc. were responsible for the teaching. It was an international gathering and Pastors from Europe ministered, e.g. Pastor Theodore Monod (France) and Pastor Stockmeyer (Switzerland) according to the official Minutes. In September, 1874, *The Christian's Pathway to Power* records, that hotels and lodging houses in Oxford had agreed to a reduction of their fees. An Irish Minister, the Rev. W. J. McCormick of Kilbride, Arklow, was present and commented, that he had previously thought the views of Boardman, etc. were "visionary and unpractical". He decided to go to the Union Meetings and he wrote subsequently, "Never can I be too thankful that I was led by God to meet Him at Oxford". An anonymous person testified, according to the Oxford Minutes, "The week at Oxford was happy, but it was the happiness of hope, this has been the happiness of rest". Oxford was to be a decisive event in the providence of God.

The Brighton Conference was another occasion of great blessing to all who attended. Every public building was put at the disposal of the Conference by the Town Council – free of charge. Early pillars of Keswick, among them, the Rev. Prebendary H.W. Webb-Peploe of St Paul's, Onslow Square, London ministered at the Conference. Pearsall Smith's last words at Brighton on 8th June, 1875, were, "The Brighton Conference has ended and the blessings from the Convention have begun".

However, a disaster occurred when Pearsall Smith was accused of being over friendly to a young lady who had come to him for counselling. Recent documentary evidence reveals that the accusation was without very much foundation, but in Victorian days, any perception of scandal was enough. *The Brighton Weekly* (cited by N. Scotland) reported the incident under the headline, "Famous American Evangelist Found in Bedroom of Adoring Female Follower". Historian Hylson-Smith suggests, that Pearsall Smith's "fall from grace was swift and irreparable. It called into question the plausibility of the new teaching and brought the issue of antinomianism to the fore". Smith was told by eight friends that he should leave Britain and he did forthwith! In correspondence from Smith, discovered in the 1960s, he protested his innocence. R.P. Smith's life simply fell apart after the incident and in 1894 his granddaughter, Alys, married the atheistic philosopher, Bertrand Russell. Walter Sloan commented about Mr Smith, "In him the Convention lost one who was perhaps its most used instrument".

It was at the Oxford Union Meetings that the Rector of St. John's Parish Church, Keswick, Canon Harford-Battersby was especially blessed and moved by God to call, what was to become known as the Keswick Convention in 1875. His decision was to lead directly, and 39 years later, to the formation of the North of Ireland Keswick Convention. As Rowlandson, a former Keswick Council Secretary wrote, commenting about the effect of Oxford upon Harford-Battersby, "The Canon was fired with new spiritual life and soon all Britain would feel the recoil".

# Chapter 4

# The Rev. Canon T.D. Harford-Battersby and the first Keswick Convention

To understand the purpose, structures and ministry of the North of Ireland Keswick Convention it is important to trace the personal story of the Rev. Canon Harford-Battersby (1822-1888), the founder of the Keswick Convention.

Harford-Battersby went up to Balliol College, Oxford as an evangelical and, while there, he imbibed the teachings being presented to the Church of England by John Henry Newman. He wrote (cited by Hartford-Battersby & Moule) "with regard to their practical teaching, I must say that, I think (the Newmanists) are generally most unjustly and unreasonably abused, they have introduced a far higher standard of holy living". While serving as curate in Gosport, Hampshire (1847-1849) he came across F. Myer's book, *Catholic Thoughts* (1848). Myer was Rector of Keswick and, eventually, Harford-Battersby joined him as a colleague. He wrote in his diary on 19th October, 1849, "I am persuaded on the whole of the truth of Protestant principles;

Anglo-Catholicism I believe to be inconsistent and untenable by an honest mind". Harford-Battersby returned to his evangelicalism adopting Myers's concern for his people, the Church and its unity. Hartford-Battersby & Moule comment:

> Mr Battersby became more and more convinced that only by uniting with others … could work be done that should be both widespread and lasting. His great idea was to bring people together. Wherever he looked, he saw disunion and isolation, and their attendant evils, coldness and inactivity.

The Canon also became concerned about world mission and, with a Mr Townsend, he visited missionary gatherings throughout the Lake District. He wrestled too with his own spiritual life, looking for reality and power. Writing about his frustrations in his diary on 30th October, 1853, he commented that he was far from, "enjoying the peace and love and joy habitually which Christ promises". Harford-Battersby, aware of the holiness movement, did not take Pearsall Smith's and W.E. Boardman's teaching in an uncritical manner. *The Christian* in 1874 carried a series of articles by Pearsall Smith entitled 'Holiness by Faith'. The Canon was impressed by "the unusually high level of Christian experience which the writer seemed to be enjoying", although he was aware of some dangerous unguarded statements and claims being made.

While on holiday in Silloth on the Solway Firth, Canon Harford-Battersby met and shared some ministry with the Rev. William Haslam, a well-known evangelist. As already noted, many sections of the church in Britain at that time were examining the holiness movement and both men talked extensively about the doctrine of sanctification. The Rev. Dr Elder Cumming of Glasgow, a later Keswick worthy, knew them both and wrote:

> Mr Haslam had been for years, even then, teaching the doctrines of holiness; and, doing so in meetings at Silloth, found in Canon Battersby an unwilling and somewhat prejudiced listener. Several conversations on the subject brought them no nearer to each other; and the result was a suggestion by Mr Haslam, that Canon Battersby should attend a convention which was to be held shortly at Oxford.

It was at Oxford in 1874, that the Canon's life was radically changed and to use his own words, he "passed from a seeking to a resting faith". Upon his return to Keswick he recounted his experiences at Oxford to the usual Friday evening prayer meeting at St. John's. One member present spoke of, "the glow which seemed to overspread his face telling without any words that some new secret had indeed illuminated his life". He had been so blessed at Oxford that he had to make it known to others.

Canon Harford-Battersby was Secretary of the Annual Conference of the Evangelical Union of the Diocese of Carlisle and on September 29th 1874, a lecture prepared by him about Oxford was read at their meeting in Kendal. It was presented by his friend, Mr Robert Wilson, because Harford-Battersby was ill at the time. In the lecture entitled "Higher Attainments of Christian Holiness and how to promote them", he thanked God, "that He seems now to be calling His Church specially to betake herself of her Sovereign Lord and Head, in order to claim her undoubted heritage of power and blessing". Harford-Battersby related the impact that Oxford had upon himself:

> And so vivid was the sense of God's presence at these meetings ...
> that a new era of blessing was about to dawn upon the Church of
> God, in which the power of God would afresh be manifested in an
> extraordinary degree.

However, the Oxford Union Meetings had been viewed with suspicion by some of those who were considered to be the leaders of the evangelical wing of the Church of England. Among them was a personal friend of Harford-Battersby, the Very Rev. Dean Close of Carlisle, with whom he had laboured in the cause of evangelical truth. Harford-Battersby was opening himself to the charge of countenancing unscriptural errors. In his lecture of 29th September, Harford-Battersby was firm in his conviction that the living of a holy life involved both understanding what we are in Christ and, that it also involved the human will. He was anxious to declare that he did not believe in "perfectionism" or "the delusion that there is no longer any sin is us".

After the Brighton Conference also, severe criticisms of the holiness teaching were made by the Rev. J.C. Ryle and others. Ryle commented that the difference between the Oxford and Brighton Conferences and Moody's preaching was like that between "sunshine and fog". In his book *Holiness* (1877) he denounces the idea of holiness by faith and writes about the life in Christ as being dominated by strife and declares that the Christian is, "a man of war", as he wrestles against sin. Ryle was a leader in the evangelical party of the Church of England and was consecrated first Anglican Bishop of Liverpool in 1880. Mr R.P. Smith's fall and subsequent departure did not help and attracted a lot of suspicion and adverse comment!

Undeterred by his critics and by comments about the fall of Pearsall Smith, Harford-Battersby and Mr Robert Wilson from Cockermouth convened what they called 'The Three Days Union Meetings for the Promotion of Practical Holiness' at Keswick, to begin on 29th June, 1875. "Union" because it was hoped to unite people from various church traditions in the pursuit of God and all that He had for them. The principal speaker was to have been Mr Pearsall Smith but of course that was impossible. The Christian press carried the following notice:

> THREE DAYS' UNION MEETINGS FOR THE PROMOTION OF PRACTICAL HOLINESS – Christians of every section of the church of God are cordially invited to attend the meetings for the above object which it is proposed to be held at Keswick, on Tuesday June 29th, and the two following days. Many, we are sure, are everywhere thirsting for a deeper draught of the Water of Life, and anxiously enquiring how they may be brought to envoy more of the Divine presence in their daily life, and a fuller manifestation of the Holy Spirit's power, whether in subduing the lusts of the flesh, or in enabling them to offer more effective service to their God. It is certainly God's will and desire that His children should be satisfied in regard to these longings of their souls, and there are those who can testify that He has satisfied them, and that He does satisfy them with daily fresh manifestations of His grace and power. To give opportunities for such testimonies, and for their exposition more especially in the Scriptures of the Truth in their bearing upon this important subject, we, the undersigned, in dependence on the Divine blessing, have resolved to convene the above meetings, and we implore all who are interested in the welfare of the church of Christ, and in the advancements of practical holiness, to unite with us in earnest prayer for the guidance of the Holy Spirit in all arrangements for these meetings, and for His blessing on the teaching and testimonies of God's servants. – T.D. HARFORD-BATTERSBY, St. John's Parsonage, Keswick; ROBERT WILSON, Broughton Grange, Cockermouth.

Attendees were to come to Keswick desiring to know God. They were to prepare themselves for every meeting with prayer. They were to take sufficient sleep and be careful about their diets. Any conversations that were not helpful to the seeking for God were to be avoided, as were matters of theological dissension. The official programme, when studied today, seems very mechanical. Evil was to be renounced and with an open mind people were to come to hear God's Word. Robert Wilson, the Cockermouth Quaker, supplied the motto "All One in Christ Jesus" and three flags fluttered from the marquee poles in the Vicarage garden with "Love", "Joy" and "Peace" printed upon them. Dr J. Edwin Orr comments about the 1859 Revival and Keswick:

> Keswick borrowed its evangelical ecumenism, with its slogan "All One in Christ Jesus", from the revival of 1858-59 and the movements which followed from it. Unlike certain other products of the revival, the Keswick Convention maintained its evangelical and evangelistic character.

The ministry, which was a mixture of Bible teaching and personal testimony, was delivered by Revs Canon Harford-Battersby, Prebendary H.W. Webb-Peploe, T. Philips, G.N. Thornton and Messrs H.F. Bowker, T.M. Croome and Mr Shirley. Mrs Compton was responsible for the ministry to Ladies.

Harford-Battersby, in a letter dated 12th July, 1875 and published by *The Christian's Pathway to Power* on 2nd August, wrote:

> On Tuesday, Wednesday, Thursday and Friday, we met at 7am for prayer and praise, and truly refreshing were those morning hours, when the dew of heaven fell so abundantly on the spirits of some 300 or 400 worshippers who gathered at those times to wait upon the Lord. ... In the evenings the tent, which held rather under than 1,000 people, was crowded, and many outside loitered even in pouring rain.

The climax of the Convention was reached on Thursday 1st July, when the Holy Spirit was the subject and personal testimonies were given. Harford-Battersby comments in his letter of 12th July, 1875:

> There is a remarkable resemblance in the character of these testimonies – the most striking of them - as to the nature of the blessing received, viz. the ability given to make a full surrender to the Lord, and the consequent experience of an abiding peace, exceeding far anything previously experienced.

Johnson suggests that teaching given at Keswick under Harford-Battersby's direction was "more wisely managed" and that he gave "more cautious leadership" than Pearsall Smith had done in other places.

The Keswick Convention has met every year since 1875 apart from 1940 and it has spread to become an evangelical event in many countries worldwide. In 1876, the planners of Keswick conducted a Convention in Dublin.

Chapter 5

# The Irish Connection

A s already indicated Keswick made its way to Ireland in 1876 when a Convention was held in Dublin. It was organised by the leaders of the Convention in Cumbria. *The Irish Times* of 25th October, 1876 carried the following advertisement:

### Dublin Convention for the Deepening of Spiritual Life
### 20th -23rd November 1876

| | |
|---|---|
| Rev. T. Monod | Rev. H.W. Williamson |
| Rev. Dr Mackey | Canon Harford-Battersby |
| Rev. D. Barnado | Rev. Dr Craig |
| Rev. Prof. Smyth MP | Rev. J. Donnelly |
| Rev. A.S. Windle | Rev. Dr McCarthy |
| Rev. Dr S. Patterson | Mr T.B. Smithies |

Notice that the Revs T. Monod and Canon Harford-Battersby shared in the ministry. Irish preachers were also used and among them were the Rev. H.W. Williamson, Minister of Fisherwick Presbyterian Church, Belfast and the Rev. Professor R. Smyth MP of Magee College, Londonderry. At the 1891 and 1893 Dublin Conventions, Mr Robert Wilson, the Keswick Convention Secretary, was one of the Speakers and in 1894 the Rev. Dr H.C.G. Moule, Principal of Ridley Hall, Cambridge participated. Dr Moule was to be appointed Bishop of Durham in 1901 and his evangelical and scholarly connections did much for the prestige of the Keswick Movement. Other Conventions were held around the greater Dublin area in the last decade of the nineteenth century. The Kingstown (now Dun Laoghaire) Convention, for example, began in 1895 and the North Dublin Convention in 1899.

A Belfast Convention was held in 1887, when the ministry was brought by the Revs Evan Hopkins, Hudson Taylor and others. Mr Robert Wilson was a Speaker at the 1888 and the 1890 Belfast Conventions. He was well-known in Belfast in those days and was to have a massive influence over Amy Carmichael, the well-known Irish missionary to India who received confirmation of her call to service at the Keswick Convention of 1892. Robert Wilson was known to her family as the DOM, the "dear old man". Amy had been greatly challenged at the Keswick Convention in Glasgow in 1886 and then during the Belfast Convention of 1887. Her story, and that of the Dohnavur Fellowship, is well documented in her biography written by Bishop Frank Houghton in 1953 and entitled, *Amy Carmichael of Dohnavur*. In 1888 and 1890, the Rev. Dr F.B. Meyer, the leading nonconformist Minister of the day, was one of the Speakers at the Belfast Convention. Keswick, its distinctive spirituality and its major Speakers were well-known throughout Ireland at the turn of the twentieth century.

However, the largest 'Keswick style' Meetings were held at Fenaghy, near Cullybackey, Co. Antrim in August 1887, July 1889 and July 1892. From photographic evidence they were held under the Keswick banner "All One in Christ" and they certainly followed the general Keswick approach. *The Ballymena Observer* of 6th August, 1887 gave the purpose of the meetings; "to unite in prayer for the outpouring of the Holy Spirit on the district and land, for the preaching of the everlasting Gospel, and for a conference regarding the evangelisation of the heathen". Tents for Foreign Mission Meetings, for the Deepening of Spiritual Life and for Inquirers etc. were erected in the field. Literature was provided by two Ballymena booksellers; there were refreshment stalls and the praise, including hymns, was led by the Ballymena YMCA Choir. The meetings were held on the land of the local mill owner Mr William Young. The same edition of *The Ballymena Observer*, commenting on the location of the meetings, recorded:

> To those who do not know Fenaghy it may be well to say that the field selected is one of the most suitable for speaking purposes. It rises with unbroken regularity like an amphitheatre from the edge of the Maine water until it touches the road leading to Ballymena. It is very spacious too for the tents in which the various sectional meetings are to be held.

The meetings were called the 'Fenaghy Camp Meetings' and the use of the word 'Camp' suggests a link to the holiness movement. The first Fenaghy Meetings were held on 10th and 11th August, 1887. Megaw writes that 79 shopkeepers in Ballymena closed to facilitate the meetings in 1887 and 57 of them closed on Wednesday and Thursday afternoons in 1889. Mary Crawford Brown, writing in *Woman's Work,* a Presbyterian Missionary Magazine of October, 1892, summarised an address given by the Rev. William Park at Fenaghy and mentions the thousands who gathered there. *The Ballymena Observer* of 13th August, 1887, mentions between 5,000 and 7,000 people being in attendance.

Well-known Christian leaders were invited to preach. For example, in 1887 it was hoped that the Rev. Charles Haddon Spurgeon would be the main Speaker. He was contacted and his reply is cited by Megaw:

> Westwood, Beulah Hill,
> Upper Norwood.
> 1887 July 16
>
> Dear Sir,
> I wish I could come to you. But the request almost amuses me. Do you really think that I am waiting about for work, or hanging on a nail to be taken down at a few days notice? Why, my dear Sir, I never have a leisure day. When the year begins, it is usual to have every day allotted down to its close, and all arranged to be used if the Lord will.
> Engagements for the week you seek have been made so long ago that I cannot tell you when, and the year 1888 is already in great part allotted unless I go to heaven.
> It is always impossible for me to leave home at short notice; and indeed, the work of the Lord at home will not often allow for my absence at all.
> Yours very heartily,
> C.H. Spurgeon
>
> (PRONI: D 1364/M/19E).

The official programme of the Meetings at Fenaghy in 1889 indicates that three special trains were put on from Belfast to arrive at Cullybackey for the 11:00am meeting. Trains from Portrush, Cookstown and Derry also conveyed attendees to the meetings. *The Ballymena Observer* of 19th July, 1889, reported that not less than 10 to 12,000 people were present. In 1892 because of the General Election, only two speakers were invited, namely, Mr DL Moody and the Rev. John McNeill of Regent Square Presbyterian Church,

London. Unfortunately the illness of Moody's son meant that he could not come and "his place was filled by other eminent speakers", according to *The Ballymena Observer* of 24th July, 1892.

Well-known Christian missionaries and leaders participated at Fenaghy. Among them was Reginald Radcliffe (1825-1895), a Liverpool Solicitor, evangelist in the 1859 Revival and close friend of Hudson Taylor. Taylor himself ministered at Fenaghy as did General Sir R. Phayre K.C.B., aide de Camp to Queen Victoria and a Vice President of the Anglo-Indian Evangelisation Society. Lord Radstock, Granville Augustus William Waldegrave, 3rd Baron Radstock (1833-1913), a Missionary statesman who had been involved in the Great Russian Awakening (1873-1884), participated. In addition, local Ministers, such as the Rev. Dr Stuart of Waterside Presbyterian Church, Londonderry, and the well-known author and Presbyterian Minister the Rev. W.J. Paton whose books were read far and wide also preached. Mr James Barton, an Anglican from Dundalk, also participated. He was a member of St. Nicholas Parish Church, a local landowner and member of the Institute of Civil Engineers who devoted his professional life to building the Irish Railways, supervising the building of the Boyne Viaduct and the Greenore harbour.

The Rev. HM Williamson, Minister of Fisherwick Presbyterian Church in Belfast and Moderator of the General Assembly (1896-97) shared in the planning of the Meetings. He was a Referee of the Rev. Henry Grattan Guinness's 'East London Institute for Home and Overseas Missions'. Another interesting fact about the Fenaghy Meetings is that they were organised certainly in 1899 by among others, the Rev. Henry Montgomery who in 1914 was to be appointed as the Chairman of the North of Ireland Keswick Convention's Committee. His brother, Mr S.G. Montgomery was part of the Fenaghy planning team and he was to become a member of the first North of Ireland Convention Committee.

In addition to the Conventions and Meetings already mentioned, there were other significant Conventions in Ireland in 1914. *The Belfast News Letter* of 23rd June, 1914, reporting on the first North of Ireland Keswick Convention, indicates that "The South, East and West of Ireland had their Conventions and there had not been one in the North".

In the South, the Convention had met in Killarney from 1905. Meeting first in the Lake Hotel it later moved to a 900 seater tent as The *Life of Faith* of 12th June, 1917 reports. Its founder was Mr J.D. Crosbie of Ballyheigue Castle who in 1913 encouraged the founders of the Northern Convention and acted as its Chairman in 1914. The Speakers at the first Southern Convention were: Revs

J.S. Holden, Harrington Lees and Captain Tottenham, the Keswick Convention Treasurer who acted as Chairman. The Killarney Convention of 1906 was a significant enough event to permit the holding of a Report Meeting, according to the *Irish Times* of 31st May, 1906, in the large hall of the Dublin YMCA Upper Sackville Street on the same day and under the chairmanship of the Right Hon. the Lord Langford KCVO.

The Western Convention was held first in 1905 in the Great Southern Hotel, Mulranney, Co. Mayo. A Keswick 'Prayer Circle' had existed there as early as 1903. Like Killarney, Mulranney is located in an area of outstanding natural beauty on the northern shore of Clew Bay. *The Life of Faith* of 15th May, 1905 records, that the principal Speaker was Dr White and that details could be obtained from Mr Robert Vesey Stoney DL JP, Rosturk Castle, Mulranney. The Stoney family, like the Crosbies, were members of the Anglo-Irish Ascendancy and a member of the family, Mr James Butler Stoney (1814-1897), was a leader in the early Brethren Movement.

The Eastern Convention, met in Kingstown as early as 1895 and its Chairman was the Dr H.W. Mackintosh, the distinguished Professor of Zoology in Trinity College, Dublin. He acted as Chairman until 1924, when Mr Walter B. Sloan was appointed. Unlike the Western and the Southern Conventions the Eastern (Kingstown) Convention met until 1937. From 1938 the Convention was transferred to Greystones and continued intermittently until 1995, as its Minutes assert.

The connection with the Keswick 'Prayer Circle' ministry is clear to be seen when one considers the locations of the Irish Conventions. *The Life of Faith* encouraged this ministry by giving specific and regular prayer requests relevant to each Convention. The Southern, Eastern and Western Conventions were all mainstream Keswick Conventions, stressing the fulness of Christ for every believer and the availability of the resources of God for consecrated living. Leading Keswick Speakers were employed in their ministries. It is clear that large crowds gathered at the three locations. There can be no doubt that they made a contribution to the spiritual life of the country at the time.

In 1913, when Canon O. W. Scott and Mr R.H.S. Richardson began to think and plan for a Keswick in the North, they were not introducing anything new to the Church in Ireland and when they placed adverts for the first Northern Convention in *The Irish Times*, they expected to appeal to a wide constituency, many of whom were familiar with Keswick and its distinctive spirituality.

# Chapter 6

# Major Convention Personalities 1914-1946

The North of Ireland Keswick, as we have already noted, was the brainchild of the Rev. Canon Oswald W. Scott and Mr R.H. Stephens Richardson. When the first Convention was held in June, 1914, they had gathered a formidable team around them. I cannot possibly, in the course of this book, give a detailed biographical note about all the Convention's leaders but I do intend here to cover a number of major ones.

## Mr James Dayrolles Crosbie, DL:

Mr Crosbie was a Trustee of the Keswick Council and the Founder and Chairman of the South of Ireland Keswick. He was appointed High Sherriff of Co. Kerry in 1894. After a time of service with the Royal Welsh Fusiliers, he resigned his commission in 1897 upon the death of his elder brother. Crosbie was a liberal Landlord, selling 6,519 acres to his tenants under the Wyndham, Land Purchase (Ireland) Act (1903), while keeping possession of the Castle and demesne. The Act, one of a series of effective Irish Land Acts, was generous to tenants because the Landlord assisted the tenants to purchase their holdings. Mr Crosbie's home, Ballyheigue Castle, was destroyed by fire in 1921 during the Irish War of Independence. A Golf Course surrounds its remains today.

J.D. Crosbie chaired the North of Ireland Keswick Convention at Portstewart in 1914. He was called to the defence of the Empire in 1915; appointed a Brigadier General, winning the DSO in 1917 and the GMG in 1919. He ended his military career after serving as Base Commandant at Archangel, Russia, under the command of Field Marshall W. E. Ironside. From 1928 he lived at Muircambus House, Kilconguhar, Fife, Scotland and served as a member of the Fife County Council from 1929-1945 and as its Chairman for six years. He died in 1947 in his 83rd year. MacMahon records, "he was well-known all over Scotland for his public works. It was a happy day for Fife when he took up residence in the county in 1928".

## The Rev. Canon Oswald W. Scott:

At the first meeting of the Convention Committee on 12th September 1913, Canon O.W. Scott and Mr R.H. Stephens Richardson were appointed as Joint Honorary Secretaries. Before becoming Rector of Gilford, he had been involved in Church planting in the University area of Belfast, founding the All Saint's Parish Church and also ministering at Inver, Larne (1899-1904). Following his time at Gilford he became Rector of St. Paul's, Belfast from 1915 till 1932. God had brought Richardson and Scott together, rooting them in the same general geographical area and implanting the desire in them both, to form a Keswick Convention in the North of Ireland. Scott was committed to Keswick Teaching and spoke at the Dublin Convention in 1921, with the Rev. Gordon Watt, H.P. Ferguson and Canon J.W. Cooke, as *The Irish Times*, of 14th November, 1921, states. Canon Scott's daughter according to *The Belfast Telegraph* of 4th May, 1936, married the Rector of Portglenone, the Rev. C.A. Bateman.

His succinct history of the North of Ireland Convention, written in 1934 is an account of its first 21 years. The Convention Minute of 28th June, 1934, states:

> The Portstewart Convention Committee desire to place on record their high appreciation and their very grateful acknowledgements of the historical story of the Convention as prepared by the Rev. Canon Scott MA .... and heartily thank their colleague for the valuable services he has rendered to the Convention Movement, in Ulster and much further afield.

Canon Scott was a dearly beloved Pastor, and when St. Paul's, Belfast was reopened after the disastrous fire of 5th January, 1934, the parishioners installed a stained glass window depicting 'The Rock of Ages' in his memory. He died on Sunday 3rd May, 1936, in the early evening, after conducting the Morning Service in St. Anne's Cathedral, Belfast at which he administered

Holy Communion. The Memorial Tribute, adopted by the Convention Committee on 6th May, 1936, at a specially convened meeting, was as follows:

> Canon Scott was a man greatly beloved by all who knew him; his courtesy, his kindliness, his unselfishness and his loyalty endeared him to a wide circle of friends. But he was especially valued as a promoter and constant supporter of the Portstewart Convention Movement in Ulster. Beloved and trusted by all his colleagues, his wisdom and insight made him an invaluable helper of the Committee through the entire history of the Movement. His devoted Christian character was an outstanding quality which rendered him one of the greatest assets of the Convention. His prayer life was unique, and in his passing the Convention has lost one of its most constant remembrancers at the Throne of Grace.

The fact that the Committee had met was recorded in *The Belfast Telegraph* of 7th May, 1936. At the evening Service in St. Anne's Cathedral on 3rd May, the Very Rev. Dean W.H. Kerr said, according to *The Belfast Telegraph* of 4th May, 1936, "Canon Scott was a real man of God, closer to the sanctuary than most men, and one could feel the reality of his life, the beauty of character and the real sincerity of his devotion to the Master". The father of the author of this book belonged to St Paul's and was deeply encouraged and influenced by the ministry of Canon Scott. *The Belfast Telegraph* of 5th May, 1936, records, that Canon Scott was also a vice president of the 'Church of Ireland Young Men's Association'.

## Mr Richard Henry Stephens Richardson DL:

Mr Richardson, an evangelical Quaker, was Joint Honorary Secretary of the North of Ireland Keswick Convention from 1914 until 1919. He was appointed Deputy Chairman on 10th October, 1917, and permanently as Chairman on 18th February, 1920, a post he held with distinction until 1957.

The Richardson family had been closely connected to the Irish Linen industry since 1654. They had come from Warwickshire, England during the reign of James I and eventually formed a great linen dynasty in the North of Ireland. One of R.H. Stephens Richardson's ancestors, a Captain Nicholson, fought in the Parliamentary Army in the English Civil War. In *Young's Tour of Ireland 1776 – 1779*, it is recorded, "many Quakers, who are [take them all in all] the

34

most sensible class of people in that kingdom ... are the only wealthy traders in the island".

From the middle of the nineteenth century, the Quakers in Ireland began to take an interest in politics. Jonathan Richardson (1811-1869), "a strong Conservative and a member of the Carlton Club" was elected the Member of Parliament for Lisburn, Co. Antrim in 1857. He was the grandfather of R.H. Stephens Richardson. In 1880 James N. Richardson, was elected Liberal Member of Parliament for Co. Armagh. The history of the Richardson family is littered with soldiers, Justices of the Peace and Deputy Lord Lieutenants. John Grubb Richardson (1815-1890) inherited the family businesses and conceived the idea of the Bessbrook Model Village, shaping it to his Quaker and Temperance ideals. Until 1845, the Richardsons had been involved in the bleaching and warehousing of linen products and after 1845 they also became manufacturers of linen. Bessbrook was built on a "3 P's" principle and was to have no Public house, no Police station and no Pawnshop. The village was planned along the lines of a William Penn settlement in the USA and later inspired the Cadbury family in 1893, to begin their now famous garden township of Bourneville near Birmingham. By 1945, Bessbrook was a thriving town of nearly 3,000 people. The granite pillar in front of the weaving shop in Bessbrook asserts that the linen trade was carried on at Bessbrook as early as 1760 by the Pollock family who sold the business to the Nicholson family in 1802. John Grubb Nicholson bought it in 1845 and was sole owner from 1863 to 1878, at which date it became the property of the Bessbrook Spinning Co. Ltd. In 1882, he refused a Baronetcy from Her Majesty Queen Victoria on a point of principle.

Mr R.H. Stephens Richardson DL of Drumlyn, Moyallan inherited much of the family quality and their business interests, was the Chairman of J.N. Richardson, Sons and Owden Ltd, and of The Bessbrook Spinning Company Ltd. He was converted at age 19 on 1st March, 1889, through the ministry of his uncle, the Rev. George Grubb, who had preached at Keswick in 1886, 1888, 1889, 1892, 1895 and 1896. Rowlandson describes G. Grubb as a wild Irishman and a Keswick Speaker who did much, with others, to promote Keswick internationally. Mr Richardson was also identified with the Cripples Institute in Belfast and Bangor, Co. Down. However, as Plum comments, he was "best known as Chairman of the Portstewart Convention, which has the same objectives as the world famous Convention at Keswick in the English Lake District".

In addition to his connection with the North of Ireland Keswick Convention, which was well supported by Quakers, the Richardson family since the early years of the century "held a mini convention on the same lines in the grounds of their home in Moyallan". Missionary interest among young people was advanced at Moyallan and several people were called to full-time Missionary service. Among them was Herbert O. Pritchard, who went to India with the Regions beyond Missionary Union in 1937 and Rita Green who was called to serve with the Egypt General Mission in the same year. Mr Arthur Chapman relates this activity and also writes about the Missionary Auxiliary set up on 12th July 1939, to "support, these Campers by prayer and giving". Mr and Mrs H.O. Pritchard spoke at the Portstewart Convention Missionary Meeting in 1946, 1952, 1958, 1968, 1971 and 1983. The Moyallon Camp provided an alternative to the Orangeman's Day parades on 12th July and taught Scriptural holiness. R.H. Stephens Richardson invited Keswick Speakers to the mini convention at his own expense. It became "The Moyallon Youth Camp" from 1934 -2001.

Apart from his business and Convention links, R.H. Stephens Richardson was active in many Quaker and other interdenominational efforts as witnessed by the work at Drumgask etc.. When R. H. Stephens Richardson retired as Chairman of the Portstewart Convention, he sent a Farewell Speech to be read at the Convention Meetings on 22nd June, 1957. In it, he recounts the early life of the Convention and concluded by quoting the well-known founder of Quakerism, George Fox, who married Margaret Fell (nee Askew), the widow of Judge Thomas Fell, one of his wealthiest supporters, "I am nothing. Christ is all". Mr Richardson used as a text for his farewell Address, "The wall shall be built in perilous times" (Daniel 9:25). Having the name of "Richardson" so closely associated with the Convention ensured its connection with the core of Ulster Protestant society, as well as its business and manufacturing life from 1914 until 1957.

R.H. Stephens Richardson was very conscious of the situation in which the Convention was ministering and it was the practice of the Convention to send royal greetings to the Monarch each year. In 1922, while chairing a Convention Meeting, he was informed that Field Marshall Sir Henry Wilson had been assassinated outside his home in London, by Irish terrorists. He asked the Rev. Dr Alexander Smellie to lead the large congregation in prayer and, according to Richardson's Farewell Address, this is the text of the prayer,

In such circumstances may the people see what Thy purposes are, and lift their hearts in trust and faith ever more to Thee. May each emergency only be a fresh call to them to throw themselves on the omnipotence of God in Christ. We do pray for that stricken home, and especially for the stricken heart of the widow. Oh Father, may the everlasting arms be underneath her. May the arms of Jesus Christ be round about her, and in this hour, when her own heart and flesh faint and fail, may the Almighty and Sovereign Loving God be the strength of her heart and her portion for evermore.

## The Very Rev. Dr Henry Montgomery:

At the Committee Meeting on 13th January, 1914, it was agreed that Dr Montgomery (1847-1943) should be appointed Chairman of the General Committee, an office he held for 24 years. Henry Montgomery, one of the Secretaries of the Fenaghy Meetings had been ordained and installed as Minister of Albert Street Presbyterian Church, Belfast on 15th August, 1882. Later, he was called to begin a new work as Minister of the Shankill Road Mission and Congregation on 24th September, 1907. His work on the Shankill Road is documented elsewhere. He was a strong leader, a great philanthropist and an effective evangelist. Henry Montgomery was appointed Moderator of the General Assembly of the Presbyterian Church in Ireland in 1912 and received the honorary degree of Doctor of Divinity from the Presbyterian Theological Faculty, Ireland. The Memorial Tribute in the Convention Minutes of 30th March, 1943, praises his industry and wise leadership as he presided over the Convention's growth from several hundred attending to over two thousand. The Minute continues,

He was a man of broad and generous outlook, sane judgment, combined with wonderful faith and courage. He exemplified in his life the teaching for which the Convention stands. His interests far exceeded the bounds of our Convention, and found expression in many directions: indeed the whole Christian Church in the North of Ireland owes much to him.

At Dr Montgomery's Funeral, the Very Rev. Dr A.F. Moody, said about him,

... but though a great evangelist and a great Keswick man, Dr Montgomery was by no means a cloistered saint; he took a keen interest in politics, and was proud to recall that, being Moderator of Assembly that same year, his signature of the Ulster Covenant came immediately after that of Sir Edward Carson.

Rowlandson records, that Dr Montgomery preached at Keswick in 1919, 1920, 1922, 1923 and in 1925. The Rev. Alexander Frazer described him as "a gift from God".

## Mr Joseph McCurry:

Mr McCurry was an Anglican and Manager of the Shankill Road Branch of the Belfast Banking Company. Dr J.T. Carson suggests that he was obviously Dr Montgomery's choice as the first Convention Treasurer. He served in that capacity through the formative years of the Convention's life from 1914-1925. Under his guidance, the site was purchased, tents were obtained and the Convention Lodge was built. Joseph McCurry was a personal friend of the Very Rev. Dr Henry Montgomery and a generous supporter of several Missionary Societies. Dr Carson also suggests, perceptively, that Mr McCurry was a modest man by nature, "for his name seldom appears in the Minutes of Committee".

## Mr R. L. McKeown:

Mr McKeown joined the Committee of the North of Ireland Keswick Convention in 1917 and the Convention Minutes of 10th October, 1917 indicate that he was appointed "to assist in the work of the secretaryship". He was confirmed as Secretary in 1920 and continued in post until his death on 11th March, 1942.

Mr McKeown had served for three years as a Missionary in Nigeria with the Qua Iboe Mission from 1899, as the Qua Iboe Mission Papers indicate, and as Irish Secretary from 1902. The Convention was to have a special relationship with the Qua Iboe Mission. This is documented in an essay contained in, *Unity, Faith, Peace and Progress in Qua Iboe and Mission Africa*, written by the author of this book, and published by Mission Africa at Belfast in 2013.

R.L. McKeown was also an author, and had many contacts throughout the Protestant community because the Qua Iboe Mission was locally based and enjoyed widespread support. After his death the Memorial Tribute in the Convention Minutes of 27th March, 1942, includes:

> R.L. McKeown who for the past 25 years has not only acted as one of the Secretaries, but has taken a leading part in the promotion of all that the Keswick Teaching at Portstewart stands for. By tongue and pen and by a deeply consecrated life he has, during a long

period of years, set an example of Christian consecration seldom attained.

In addition to his Missionary and Convention work, R.L. McKeown was one of the chief organisers of 'The Ulster United Prayer Movement'. The position enjoyed by the Convention in the war years was such that the Committee initiated and conducted at least one Province wide Day of Prayer.

When Mr McKeown died, a joint Memorial Service was held for him and Mr Samuel Alexander Bill MBE, the founder of the Qua Iboe Mission, on 29th March, 1942. The Qua Iboe Council Minutes of 16th March, 1942, record that, most of the participants were members of both the Portstewart Convention Committee and the Qua Iboe Mission Council, with the Very Rev. Dr Henry Montgomery delivering the Message.

In addition, R.L. McKeown had been a foundation member of Oldpark Presbyterian Congregation, Belfast and was ordained as an Elder when the Congregation was established on 22nd November, 1906, and acted as Session Clerk, from 1939 – 1942. Oldpark Congregation was ministered to successively by the Revs William McCoach (1902 - 1933), and Dr James Dunlop (1933 -1973). Both men were to serve as members of the Convention Committee; Mr McCoach from 1918 and Dr Dunlop from 1937. Their close relationship with Mr McKeown was influential in the Convention's pre-war development and ministry. R. L. McKeown's two sons became Presbyterian Ministers, the Rev. Charles Herbert McKeown and the Rev. Stanley McKeown. His daughter, Elizabeth Florence became Professor of Morbid Anatomy at the Queen's University, Belfast, and a Consultant Pathologist.

## The Very Rev. Dean J.W. Cooke:

J.W. Cooke, a foundation member of the Convention Committee, succeeded Canon Scott as one of the Honorary Convention Secretaries in 1936. He held the position until 1954. He assisted in the leading of praise at the Convention. J.W. Cooke served as Rector of Dromore Cathedral, of Christ Church, College Square, Belfast and Dean of Connor from 1945. He was a man of great personal devotion and an effective preacher. He loved the Keswick Movement and proclaimed its message at local Conventions in N. Ireland.

## Mr Montserrat Henry Walker, JP:

Mr Walker was Convention Treasurer from 1925 until he died in 1933. He lived in Newtownards, Co. Down and was Managing Director of Walker,

George, & Co., Ltd, manufacturers of spinning yarns for linen weaving, twine, cords and ropes. In 1912 he was committed to the cause of the Union. He was a member of St. Mark's Parish Church in Newtownards. Dr J.T. Carson records that his life was described as "a beautiful unselfish thing". Mr Walker was committed to the Keswick message and inspired his son, Mr George M. Walker, a future Convention Treasurer, to be so also.

## Mr Robert Clyde:

Mr Clyde was a Presbyterian and a prominent business man in Northern Ireland. He was appointed Chairman of White Tomkins and Courage Ltd in 1933. A member of the Qua Iboe Mission Council, he had many contacts in the business and political life of N. Ireland. He was Convention Treasurer from 1933-1949. Mr Clyde was a generous benefactor of the Convention. His advice was often sought by and readily given to the Committee. Among other practical things, such as providing transport, he paid for the Ministers' Breakfast for many years. His contribution to the Convention cannot be over emphasised.

## Convention Office Bearers (1914-1945)
## Chairmen of the Convention

### 1914
Mr J.D. Crosbie DL (Chairman of the Killarney Convention)

### 1915 – 1916
Mr Albert A. Head, (Chairman of the Keswick Convention)
### 1917 – 1957
Mr R.H. Stephens Richardson;
(Appointed as deputy Chairman on 10th October 1917
and permanently appointed as Chairman
18th February 1920)

## Chairmen of the Convention Committee:

### 1914 – 1938
The Rev. Dr Henry Montgomery
### 1938 – 1944
Ad Hoc Chairmen due to Dr Montgomery's protracted illness
### 1944 - 1958
The Rev. James Dunlop

## Joint Honorary Secretaries of the Convention

### 1914 – 1919

Mr R.H. Stephens Richardson

The Rev. Canon O. Scott

### 1920 – 1935

Mr R.L. McKeown

The Rev. Canon O.W. Scott (died in 1936)

### 1917 – 1942

Mr R.L. McKeown

After Mr McKeown's death, Mr R.G. Bass and Miss E. Knox (Qua Iboe Mission) acted on an ad hoc basis until 1944 and the appointment of Mr J. McDonald.

### 1936-1954

The Rev. Canon J.W. Cooke

### 1944 - 1956

Mr J. McDonald

## Treasurers of the Convention:

### 1914 – 1925

Mr Joseph McCurry

### 1925 – 1933

Mr M.H. Walker

### 1933 - 1950

Mr Robert Clyde

*Fenaghy Meetings 1887, 1889 and 1892. Note: "All One in Christ".*

*1914 Convention Committee and friends. Mr R.H.S. Richardson is 3rd from left and 4th from left is Mr J.D. Crosbie; immediately behind him is the Very Rev. Dr Henry Montgomery.*

*Portstewart in 1914*

*1928 group.*

*Rev. Dr F.B. Meyer, Baptist Minister, author and international propagandist for the Keswick Movement. Preacher at Portstewart in 1919 and 1922.*

*Signatures of Revs J. Russell Howden, W.F. Fullerton, Dr F.B. Meyer, Alexander Smellie and Mr G.F. Whitehead, Speakers at the 1922 Convention.*

*The Very Rev. Dr Henry Montgomery. Convention Committee chairman from 1914-1938.*

*The Convention tent in 1926.*

*Interior of the tent from 1914 - 1998. Note Keswick motto "All One in Christ Jesus"*

*Rev. and Mrs Russell Howden. He preached at 13 Portstewart Conventions.*

*Rev. Alexander Frazer preached at 15 Portstewart Conventions.*

*The Rev. Graham Scroggie – regular Speaker in the 1920s.*

*The Right Rev. Bishop Taylor Smith was a Speaker in 1930 and in 1932.*

*Mrs R.H. Stephens Richardson, Rev. Alexander Fraser and Harrison the Richardson's chauffeur outside Cairn Moore in the 1930's. The limousine belonged to Mr Richardson.*

*A formidable Team, Mr R.G. Bass, Rev. Canon O.W. Scott, Mr R.L. McKeown and Mr R.H. Stephens Richardson*

*Rev. Sidlow Baxter, Mr G.F. Whitehead, Mr R.G. Bass, Mr Richardson, Mr R.L. McKeown, Mr Lindsay Glegg and the Rev. W. Grist at the 1936 Convention.*

*The Chairman of the Convention Committee, the Very Rev Dr Henry Montgomery and the Secretary, Mr R.L. McKeown at the 1932 Convention.*

*The Convention Lodge built as a Caretaker's Residence and Offices in 1923 at a cost of £1,400.*

*Cairn Moore bought in 1929 for £1,350 and sold in 1949 for £3,900.*

# Chapter 7

# Conventions for all (1914-1939)

I n 1914 the Convention was described by J.K. Maclean in *The Life of Faith* as "the youngest of our Conventions for the Promotion of Scriptural Holiness. The Portstewart Convention is a child of wonderful vigour and promise". And so it was! Notice the use of the phrase, "of our Conventions", reflecting as it does the Keswick Movement. Canon Scott, in his history of the Portstewart Convention, states that his desire was to bring 'Keswick' to the North of Ireland. In 1914 Keswick had become an international Movement and the first Leaders of the Portstewart Convention wanted to begin "a Keswick Movement in Ulster".

According to the Convention Minutes of 30th August, 1918, the Committee began to organize satellite Conventions in Belfast and throughout the country, "with a view of supplementing the work of the Convention it was agreed that a number of local Conventions should be held in suitable centres in Ulster ...". A Belfast Convention, proposed for November, 1919, was to have two or three Speakers, one from the Church of England and the others, from the Presbyterian Church, reflecting the relative strength of Anglicanism and Presbyterianism in the Province. In addition, and from January 1919, monthly Meetings were held in Belfast YMCA. Local Conventions were held in Portglenone, Cookstown and Magherafelt. The Convention Minute of 27th June, 1918, records, that the Rev. Dr Charles Inwood was coming to Ireland and that "invitations had already been received from Cookstown, Omagh, Portadown, and other places were mentioned". Notice, "invitations had been received" i.e. although the Convention Committee was not asking to convene Conventions in those locations, they were often invited to do so. An appetite for Convention ministry had been created! In 1921, according to the Minute of 7th January under the heading 'Ormiston',

> Mr Toland asked for permission to hold a local Convention at Ormiston under the auspices of the Portstewart Convention Committee, the Committee to help in securing Speakers. This was cordially agreed to.

'Ormiston' is a leafy suburb of East Belfast. There is no evidence that this Convention was ever held but the request does indicate a desire for Keswick Ministry. There is no doubt that the Portstewart Convention, at that time, was making a significant contribution to the lives of many people in various areas across the country.

From even a cursory look at the local Conventions as listed below, it is easy to see that the Convention Committee was keen to return to the same locations frequently. Magherafelt in Co. Londonderry was a favourite location from 1920 – 1929. The Cities of Londonderry and Armagh were locations for local Conventions too. In 1923 over 1,000 people attended the local Convention in Londonderry.

### Londonderry 6th – 8th April, 1918
Rev. Charles Inwood

### Portglenone, Cookstown, Omagh and Portadown etc.
### Mid March – Mid April, 1919
Rev. Charles Inwood

### Belfast 25th – 28th November, 1919
Speakers: Mr W. B. Sloan (Secretary of the Keswick Convention)
Revs D.M. McIntyre,
J. Russell Howden and James E. Houston

### Four Monthly Meetings in Belfast January – April, 1919
No Speakers given

### Belfast Monthly Meeting 9th January, 1920
For the Deepening of the Spiritual Life

### Belfast 10th – 11th April, 1920
Rev. Dr F.B. Meyer

### Magherafelt 9th April, 1920
Rev. Dr Henry Montgomery

### Belfast November, 1920
Cancelled due to Civil Disorder and the Curfew Law in the City

**Belfast 9th – 13th April, 1921**
Rev. Dr F.B Meyer

**Magherafelt 31st May, 1921**
Rev. Canon Cooke, Mrs Martin Cleaver, Mr Richardson
and Mr R.L. McKeown

**Magherafelt 9th April, 1923**
Revs W.R. Sloan and J.E. Davidson

**Derry and Portadown Meetings**
Convention Minutes of 26th June 1923 record Derry
attendance up to 1,500 people

**Armagh 4th – 5th February, 1926**
Revs Dr H. Montgomery and S.J. Greer

**Magherafelt and Donaghadee**
Reported in Minutes 24th June 1926

**Donaghadee 2nd – 5th April, 1927**
Mr Walker

**Armagh 6th – 10th April, 1927**
Rev. S. J. Greer – 800 attended

**Province wide Conventions March, 1928**
Donaghadee March 8th – 11th Revs Gordon Watt and R. Bird
Ballyclare March 11th – 13th Rev. Gordon Watt
Londonderry March 14th – 18th Revs Gordon Watt and J.W. Cooke
Magherafelt March 19th – 20th Rev. Gordon Watt
Armagh March 21st – 25th Revs Watt, Cooke and E.B. Cullen
Dundrum March 26th – 28th Revs Watt and W.J. Gransden
Belfast March 28th Rev. Gordon Watt

**Armagh 7th -10th April, 1929**
Revs Dr Montgomery and J.R. Belsdon

**Dundrum – no date etc. provided**

**Donaghadee 20th April, 1929**
Revs Dr McKeag, W.J. Harrison and S.J. Greer

**Magherafelt 30th April, 1929**
Revs F.C. Gibson and H. O. Connor

**Portadown 10th – 14th May, 1931**
Revs J.W. Cooke, W.J. Harrison and Dr Hugh McKeag

**Dundrum 31st May – 4th June, 1931**
Revs J.W. Cooke and R. Nevin Lyons

**Dundrum 17th – 22nd April, 1931**
Revs J. Milton Thompson, Canon Weir, and J.J. Cooksey

**Londonderry 7th February, 1932**
Mr Samuel Dickey Gordon

**Dundrum 12th – 15th May, 1933**
Rev. Canon Parkinson Hill and Capt. Reginald Wallis

**Dundrum 23rd – 27th September, 1935**
Revs J.A.G. Ainley, Nevin Lyons and James Dunlop

**Dundrum 3rd – 9th May, 1937**
Revs Parkinson Hill and J.R.S. Wilson

**Lisburn 27th February – 4th March, 1938**
Dr Hart-Davies and the Rev. J.R.S. Wilson

**Dundrum 15th – 20th May, 1938**
Revs J.R.S. Wilson and Canon Parkinson Hill

*(Source: Convention Minutes 1914 – 1939)*

Of particular note, is the Province wide Convention held in seven centres in 1928. Most of the Speakers at these local Conventions were members of the Convention Committee. Several notable exceptions were; Belfast in 1919 when Mr Walter B. Sloan was the Speaker; in 1921 when the Rev. Dr F.B. Meyer was the Speaker; the Londonderry Convention in 1932 when popular devotional author, Mr Samuel Dickey Gordon was the Speaker. One can easily understand that these local Conventions, apart from spreading Keswick Teaching, would have encouraged the attendees to come to the main Convention at Portstewart

The Committee had created a 'Movement' that was having an impact among the Protestant community throughout the whole North of Ireland. This was possible, chiefly, through the good offices of Mr R.L. McKeown, the Convention Secretary and the local Secretary of the Qua Iboe Mission. The Convention had the benefit of the assistance of the Mission office staff. For decades the Convention Committee met in the Qua Iboe office and payment was made to the Mission for services rendered. With the outbreak of war in 1939, the local Conventions organised by the Portstewart Committee came to an end and, after the war, they never restarted. It would seem that the driving force was Mr McKeown and he died in 1942.

In addition to these local Conventions, the Committee was concerned to reach young people with Keswick teaching. As early as 1919, they debated the possibility of holding youth meetings as part of the annual Convention. In 1929, the Convention Committee received a delegation of Belfast young people who brought the request that a Young People's Convention (YPC) should be formed in Belfast. Accordingly, in 1930, arrangements were set in motion to establish such a Convention. Five members of the Portstewart Convention Committee and five Belfast young people would form the General and Executive Committee of the YPC. The Portstewart members would provide advice about Speakers etc. and the young people would be responsible for finance and all other arrangements. Mr R.G. Bass, a member of the Portstewart Convention Committee and Secretary of 'The Irish Evangelisation Society', would act as Chairman. Later that year, and due to duties in England, Mr Bass was replaced by Mr Mulligan. The first Belfast YPC was held from 22nd-28th February, 1930, and the Speakers were:

Rev. J. Millar Craig, Bangor, Co. Down.

Mr Montague Goodman, London - Preacher at Keswick
(1924 and 1929)

Rev. Bryan S.W. Green B.D. - Preacher at Keswick (1931)

Rev. F. John Scroggie, London - Preacher at North of Ireland
Keswick (1929 and 1931)

The first Belfast YPC was regarded as a success and the YPC Committee was able to send 10 guineas to the Portstewart Committee. The Portstewart Minutes of 15th April, 1930 record a report from a YPC Committee member, "large numbers not hitherto attending such Conventions were present, and he knew of many cases of personal blessing".

The second Belfast YPC was smaller than the 1930 one and the Minutes of the Portstewart Convention Committee of 17th April, 1931 record that this was attributed to "to the Speakers not being so popular, to the fact that the young people did not put so much work into the organization, and to the epidemic of influenza".

In 1931, plans were laid for the third Belfast YPC and the Portstewart Secretary, Mr R.L. McKeown, informed the YPC Committee that Mr S.D. Gordon would be coming to Portstewart in June and he would also be free to preach at the YPC in February. The YPC Committee agreed. Mr Gordon was the well-known author of the series *Quiet Talks*. The other Speaker was to be the Rev. Walter McIntyre. However a contentious issue arose, sparked by an article in *The Bible League Quarterly* by its editor, the Rev. R. Wright Hay. In the January-March edition of the *Quarterly*, Mr Hay commented:

> It is grievous that Dr Gordon should have adopted a theory which has hitherto been associated only with a rationalistic school of Bible criticism. And we are deeply concerned lest his having adopted it and published it in very confident terms, may lead some who read his books to regard his view of the Book of Isaiah as the true view.

This criticism of S.D. Gordon referred to statements he had written in his book, *Quiet Talks about the Lord's Return* (1912). In theologically conservative terms, the Rev. Hay argues that the New Testament assumes that Chapters 40 – 66 of Isaiah were in fact written by the prophet and not by someone using his name. Mr Gordon had written:

> The book of Isaiah naturally divides into two parts, chapters I – xxxix and xl – lxvi. The historical allusions of each make it quite clear that the two parts belong in two periods, far apaRt One hundred and eighty years intervene between the close of the time stated in Isaiah's first chapter as his period of prophesying, and the beginning of the return from exile into which the second part fits. But the full inspiration of the second part is in no wise affected by the modestly of this rarely Spirit swayed man, who withholds his own name, and, after the manner of his time, attaches his writings to those of a well-known man of his nation.

S.D. Gordon also drew criticism from the Bible League because of a comment made in *Quiet talks about Jesus* (1906) when he wrote, "There is no cross in God's plan of atonement". Wright Hay had written a classic defence in *The Bible League Quarterly* (January – March 1932) for the centrality of the cross in God's economy of Salvation. He quotes Gordon, "It clears the ground not to have any theory about Jesus' death". Hay counters his understanding of Gordon by quoting, Luke 24:20-26; John 3:14-15; 12:32-33; 18:11; Galatians 3:13 and Hebrews 10:7-10. He then adds a comment to his defence of the Conservative view, "we pray that the above and similar Scriptures may clear the mind of all his readers of the theory that there is no cross in God's plan of Atonement".

Mr Gordon wrote a response to *The Bible League Quarterly*, (April – June, 1932:50):

My dear Mr Wright Hay,

Thank you very much for sending me this copy of the Bible League Quarterly, with its illusions to my writings.

I have a deep sorrow in my heart in noting your taking certain statements of mine without giving their setting, and which so completely ignores the essential teaching.

I am grateful that in the six months that I have had the privilege of ministering here in Old England and Scotland and Wales, so many have heard my simple messages with their emphasis. That emphasis has been mostly firmly placed on the absolute integrity of the Word of God throughout, as being fully and directly inspired by the Holy Spirit; and on the atonement of the blood atonement of our Lord Jesus, as the only means of salvation for anyone, and as the very heart of all our Christian faith.

I would be most grateful if this simple letter of mine might be given as prominent a place in your valued journal as this article of yours lying open before me.

With deep sorrow in my heart,

Believe me,

S. D. Gordon.

It should be said that S.D. Gordon's books were not closely reasoned theologically, but in the N. Ireland of 1931-2 anything that suggested the accommodation of what was known as 'Modernism' was rejected. The whole episode is to be seen against the backdrop of the "heresy trial" of the Rev. Principal J.E. Davey in 1927 and the ministry of the popular Evangelist W.P. Nicholson. Dr Davey, of the Presbyterian College, Belfast, had been acquitted by the Belfast Presbytery and the case then went by way of appeal to the General Assembly. He was also acquitted there of the charges brought against him. The charges were to do with theological matters, arising chiefly out of his books; *Our Faith in God* (1922) and *The Changing Vesture of the Faith* (1923). The Very Rev. A.A. Fulton in his biography of J.E. Davey writes, that while a younger man and attending the Keswick Convention, Davey "had a personal experience which convinced him of the reality of the presence and power of the Holy Spirit". Dr Davey's father had been an outstanding Gospel Preacher and, when Minister of 1st Ballymena Presbyterian Church, had been a member of the planning team for the Fenaghy Camp Meetings.

W.P. Nicholson had been ordained to the Christian Ministry by the Cumberland Presbyterian Church in the United States of America on 15th April, 1914. He was an effective Evangelist and, in the 1920s, his was a household name. He had been greatly blessed at a series of meetings for the deepening of the spiritual life in 1899 conducted by Keswick Speaker, the Rev. J. Stuart Holden. Nicholson preached against Liberalism, Unitarianism, Romanism, and Higher Criticism. He was particularly critical of the Presbyterian establishment. It is Fulton's opinion that, "if it had not been for the Nicholson campaigns the Trial would not have got off the ground at all". It is not my purpose here to give a history of the 1927 Heresy Trial but it is merely highlighted as part of the local scene when S.D. Gordon was invited to the Belfast YPC.

A delegation of young people (Mr Murray, Mr Ardill and Mr Paisley) from the Belfast YPC was received by the Portstewart Convention Committee on 15th January, 1932. The Minutes of the meeting record:

> Each of them made lengthy statements regarding Dr Gordon's teaching in paragraphs in his books published 20/26 years ago, and which Wright Hay had criticized, informing the Committee that they would be compelled to dissociate themselves from the Convention, unless Mr Gordon publicly repudiated the paragraphs, or his engagement as a Speaker was cancelled.

After the meeting, the Portstewart Convention Committee, believing that Mr Gordon had been misrepresented, contacted him, to ask him to clarify his views. He replied:

> I believe in the Word of God, as inspired directly and fully by the Holy Spirit through the men who wrote. This applies to the entire book, from, cover to cover.

> I believe in the deity of Jesus Christ; that He was very God of very God, born of the virgin Mary by the direct creative act of the Holy Spirit.

> I believe that Jesus Christ died for our sins on the Cross as our substitute Saviour, and only though His precious blood is there salvation for any one of all the race.

> I believe that sin is an act of rebellion against God's perfect love-will, and that it is so damnable that there is no escaping the

consequences of it except through the blood of Christ.

I believe that every man must make personal choice of Christ as his Saviour for present character and future destiny: and only so is there Salvation for him from unending death in the future world.

I believe in the Pentecostal fulness of the Holy Spirit, and through this blessed experience one may live a life of purity and holiness, in the purpose of his heart, and increasingly in social practice.

I believe that our Lord Jesus Christ is coming back again in person to bring in the Kingdom reign, and His coming is a thing to be expected in our day.

The Portstewart Convention Committee was satisfied with Gordon's statement and he joined the Speakers team in 1932, with Rev. Alexander Frazer, Rt Rev. Bishop Taylor Smith, Rev. E.W. Mills and Mr G.F. Whitehead. However, the Belfast YPC Committee was not satisfied! The link between the two was broken by the Portstewart Committee and on 9th February, 1932, their Minutes record, "This Committee [Belfast YPC] ceases to function as far as the Portstewart Movement is concerned". The YPC Committee held their 1932 Convention with the understanding that the word 'Keswick' would not appear in any of their publicity. The Belfast YPC continued to meet in the YMCA Wellington Hall, Belfast until the 1970s and the youth ministry of Portstewart from 1932 was confined to the week of the Convention in June.

There was a certain amount of 'fallout' regarding the Portstewart Convention's acceptance of S.D. Gordon's statement. One contemporary denominational magazine carried the headline "Broadness of Portstewart Convention Committee" and even suggested that they might ask Professor J.E. Davey to be a Speaker!

Later, on 6th November, 1935, the Londonderry Young People's Convention was established. This Convention was inspired by both the Portstewart Convention and the Belfast Young People's Convention and, although never part of the Portstewart Convention as such, it was called, according to its Minutes of 3rd January, 1936, "Keswick in Londonderry" from some time. Mr T.S. Mooney was appointed its first Chairman and served in that role until 1982. He was a member of the Portstewart Convention Committee from 1944 until his death in January, 1986.

The Londonderry YPC, like the Belfast YPC, did useful work in bringing young believers from all the Protestant denominations together for Keswick Teaching. The Londonderry Committee contacted all the local Congregations, Christian Endeavour Societies, Boys' and Girls' Auxiliaries, and representatives were appointed in each local church. Students at Magee University and Theological Colleges were involved and the church was marshalled for prayer. The Speakers at the first Londonderry YPC were the Rev. J.R.S. Wilson and Mr T.B. Rees. The Convention was to be the catalyst for regular fellowship meetings and for joint gatherings with 'The Belfast Young People's Convention'. The union of the two Conventions was such that the Londonderry Minutes of 18th September, 1942, refer to, "the Young People's Convention Movement in our Province".

The Londonderry YPC is now a 'Bible Week' rather than a Keswick style Convention and has made and continues to make a massive contribution to the churches in the City and district. At the 2013 Convention, the Speaker was the Rev. Darran McCorriston of Ballyloughan Presbyterian Church in Ballymena. He currently serves as Speaker and Programme Convener on the 'Keswick at Portstewart' Committee.

# Chapter 8

# Property Owners (1914 - 1946)

T he first North of Ireland Keswick Convention presented its organisers with a logistic nightmare. Having decided to meet in Portstewart in June 1914, they needed a tent, somewhere to erect it and seats for the attendees. With faith and a lot of business acumen, they set about hiring a tent, renting a site and having benches made for seating the people.

## Large Marquee:

Mr Rea, a well-known Gospel preacher, offered his tent but, after some discussion, it was agreed to hire a suitable tent from Messrs Flack of Belfast. The seating capacity was about 500 and Mr McLaughlin, a Committee member, had the necessary seats made. In 1915, because of the demands of the War, it was difficult to procure a tent but one was eventually found. In 1919 separate tents were provided for the bookstall and for a bicycle shed. In 1920, Mr Going of the Killarney Convention offered their 700 seater tent. The Portstewart Committee considered that it would be too small and steps were taken to provide their own tent. The purchase was postponed until 1921, when the offer of The Waterproofing Co., Barrhead, Glasgow was accepted at £650. The tent measured 120 feet by 60 feet and with the required site works etc., would cost approximately £1,200. In April, 1921, an Appeal was launched and by June the 1,400 appeal letters had realised £750.

The Convention Committee published a list of all the major contributors. The geographical spread of these individuals is interesting and indicates something of the wide appeal of the Convention. Among them were Mr David Irwin, Co. Longford; Mr J.J. Haughton, Co. Wexford; Mr J.A.A. Wallace DL, the

Hon. Lady Hayes, Stranraer, Scotland; Miss Hepenstal, Co. Cavan and the highest contributor was the Rev. George Moody of Buncrana Presbyterian Church, Co. Donegal who donated £50.

Rev. Moody was a frequent and generous benefactor of the Convention. In 1935 he published an autobiography and gave the Convention 1,000 copies to sell with the proceeds going to the Committee's funds. *The Belfast Telegraph* of 23rd June, 1936, described him in a Convention report as, "the father of the Convention". Well-known business people are listed among the 1921 contributors, Mr M.H. Walker, the Newtownards Mill Owner; Sir Robert Anderson, former Mayor of Belfast; Mr S.D. Bell, the Belfast tea and coffee importer; Mr Joseph C. Eaton, the Londonderry businessman and Mr Robert Temple of Magee Clothing in Donegal Town.

Such was the growth of the Convention, that following the 1925 meetings, it was decided that a larger tent was required. Dr Montgomery reported that Keswick were selling a tent with a seating capacity for 2,500 people. Nothing came of this, and according to the Minutes of 1st October, 1926, it was agreed to receive tenders for a new tent measuring 140 feet by 70 feet at a cost of approximately £750.

Mr R.G. Bass, who was responsible for the tentage, reported on 3rd March 1927, that Flack & Co. would make a tent for £600, less parts of canvas and steel bolts from the former tent amounting to £115. Four flags were to be placed atop the four poles; "Love", "Joy", "Peace" and "Hope", as at Keswick. Tragically, on the Tuesday morning of the 1927 Convention the new tent was blown down in a storm and sustained serious damage. The local Churches assisted by offering their premises for the meetings as the Convention Minute of 23rd June, 1927, records.

In 1938, the tent was damaged again in a storm and in 1939 the General Committee, reported the need of a new tent. The Committee, however, persevered with the repaired tent and in 1943 they decided to purchase a new one when the war came to an end.

## Site at Enfield Street:

In 1918, the Committee discussed the desirability of owning the Convention site. Mr Gordon, its owner, agreed to sell the field for £400, subject to an annual ground rent of £6. The site measured 187 feet by 250 feet and Mr J.A. Hanna, a Civil Engineer, was employed to draw up maps and make provision for levelling the ground and the erection of a fence. Mr William Fulton, a well-known Belfast solicitor and a Committee member, advised the Committee to negotiate a 999 year Lease at £13 per year and with permission to erect houses etc..

The purchase of the site was an important issue. It allowed the Convention to be independent of any denomination, thus ensuring its Keswick ecumenicity. It also meant that the Committee could convene the Convention on the desired dates each year, without any difficulty.

The Lease facilitated the erection of Convention Lodge with office, waiting rooms and toilets, in 1923. Built by T. McKeown & Sons of Cookstown, the Lodge cost £1,400 including £124 for plumbing by Christie of Coleraine. The Lodge was let to Mr Rae, the Portstewart Golf Club professional for an annual rent of £12. In 1924 the Lodge was then let to Miss Ferson with a rent of £20. She was to be caretaker of the property with a rebate of rent given in lieu of her duties. This arrangement continues, 90 years later, with the present tenants Mr and Mrs Roy Rainey.

## The Speaker's House

In 1914, the local Portstewart Committee set about finding a house for the Speakers. Until 1918, they were lodged in houses arranged by the Rev. Dr Montgomery and the Rev. Canon Scott. However in 1921, Miss Greer, owner of 'Cairn Moore', agreed to let the whole house and one or two other people were to be invited to join the party. The house is just across the road from the Town Hall and still bears its name above the front door in 2013. The Committee have always considered that the Speakers, because of their important and demanding role, should be accommodated in a Convention House Party. In 1929 the Committee decided to try to purchase the house when they discovered that it was going to be sold by its new owner, Mr Millar. The Committee Minute of 12th November, 1929, states:

> That the Committee of the Portstewart Convention should purchase "Cairn Moore" – (known as the Speaker's House) forthwith, and that Messrs M.H. Walker, R.G. Bass and R.L. McKeown, be and are hereby, empowered to complete same at £1,350, or as near that sum as can be effected with the owner, Mr Millar.

The house was duly purchased and, under a tenancy agreement, the YWCA made constant use of it, apart from the Convention week each year. For some time during the 2nd World War 'Cairn Moore' housed evacuees, although it was hoped that Campbell College Junior Department might have used it. In 1942 and 1943, the Convention House Party was held in 'Sunnyside' just next door to 'Cairn Moore'. Eventually, after the Speakers' House was sold for £3,900 in 1949, the House Party moved to the Links Hotel, Portstewart Other locations, including the Golf Hotel, the Windsor Hotel, Castle Erin and the Magherbouy Hotel were used. Since 2009 the TBF & KL Thompson Trust, has generously made their eminently suitable 'Rock House', Portstewart available.

# Chapter 9

# Convention Speakers 1914-1945

The Speakers between 1914 and 1945 covered a wide range of churchmanship. The denominational spread included Anglican Bishop, the Right Rev. Taylor Smith, Chaplain General to His Majesties Forces throughout the 1st World War and until 1925, and the Rev. Dr F.B. Meyer, the leading Baptist Minister. He was known to some as "Comrade Meyer" for his support of evangelical social ministry. The Rev. W.Y. Fullerton, his biographer, preached at four Portstewart Conventions. Taylor Smith preached at Portstewart in 1930 and 1932. Dr J.T. Carson writes of the Bishop, "Decorated with honours at the same time he was humble as a child. The love of Christ and the honour of his name meant more than anything else". F.B. Meyer, who had a magnetic personality and a wonderful skill in communication, came to the Convention in 1919 and 1922. Both of course preached at the Keswick Convention and Meyer was the first nonconformist to be prominent in the movement.

The Rev. Alexander Frazer, a Scottish Presbyterian came to Portstewart on 15 occasions. He was a mighty preacher who had been used by God in revival blessing in Scotland. Dr J.T. Carson's *Frazer of Tain*, is a readable and informative biography. The Rev. Charles Inwood, a Methodist, was a thorough old style Keswick man in every way. He did much to inspire and prepare for the Convention at Portstewart in 1914. He preached at our Convention on five occasions.

The Rev. W. Graham Scroggie, a Baptist and Minister of Spurgeon's Metropolitan Tabernacle during the 2nd World War, was a strong contender for "the faith once delivered to the saints". He ministered also at Charlotte

Chapel, Edinburgh and was followed there by the Rev. Sidlow Baxter. Baxter was a great favourite at Portstewart and was responsible for the Bible Readings on four occasions and on the other three, he displayed a rare novelty in his presentation of the Keswick message. Scroggie was ejected from two Congregations for his opposition to Modernism. In his later life he wrote *The Unfolding Drama of Redemption*. He came to Portstewart for the first time in 1917 and returned on five other years. The Rev. J. Russell Howden, for many years the theologian of Keswick, preached at 13 Portstewart Conventions. He was a member of the Keswick Council and preached at two of 'The Keswick in London' Conventions during the 2nd World War. Howden was involved in ministry in Shanghai, San Francisco and South Africa.

Mr G.F. Whitehead was a Quaker business man originally from Bradford and he came to Portstewart, first in 1920 and then on another unbroken 19 occasions. He was much sought after by the many Missionary house parties each year. Mr Walter B. Sloan, the Keswick Council Secretary and author of *These Sixty Years,* preached at other Irish Conventions but only once at Portstewart He had the brilliant gift of the suitable and easily remembered illustration.

Lindsay A. Glegg, was a frequent Speaker at both the Portstewart main and youth meetings in the inter war years. His first visit was in 1933 and he was invited almost every year until 1945. The Rev. Dr William Fitch preached at five Portstewart Conventions. His brother, the Rev. Dr Thomas Fitch of Ravenhill, Belfast, was a Speaker in 1949. Dr William Fitch concluded his Ministry in Knox Congregation, Toronto, at that time the largest Presbyterian Church in North America. Rev. Dr Donald Barnhouse, of 10th Presbyterian Church, Philadelphia, preached at a number of the inter war Conventions and it is of interest that one of his eminent successors, the Rev. Dr Liam Goligher, is to be a Speaker at the Centenary Convention in 2013.

In general, between 1914 and 1945, the ministry followed the traditional Keswick approach. Keswick's distinctive spirituality dominated British evangelicalism until the mid 1960s.

## Speakers at the North of Ireland Keswick Convention 1914-1945

**22nd – 27th June 1914**
Rev. Evan Hopkins
Rev. Hubert Brook
Rev. Charles Inwood
Rev. Dr Alex. Smellie
Rev. J. Chalmers Lyon

**21st – 26th June 1915**
Rev. Alexander Smellie
Rev. Canon Joynt
Rev. W.Y. Fullerton
Rev. E.L. Hamilton

**19th – 24th June 1916**
Rev. W.Y. Fullerton
Rev. E.L. Hamilton
Rev. J. Russell Howden
Rev. Dr Alexander
Smellie

**25th – 30th June 1917**
Rev. D.M. McIntyre,
Rev. J. Russell Howden
Rev. W.G. Scroggie
Rev. E L. Hamilton

**24th – 29th June 1918**
Rev. J. Russell Howden
Rev. Charles Inwood
Rev. Dr Alexander
Smellie
Mr Walter B. Sloan

**23rd – 28th June 1919**
Rev. Dr Alex. Smellie
Rev. J. Russell Howden
Rev. Dr Charles Inwood
Rev. Dr W.G. Scroggie
Rev. Dr F.B. Meyer

**21st – 28th June 1920**
Rev. J. Russell Howden
Rev. Dr W.Y. Fullerton
Rev. Gordon Watt
Rev. F.W. Ainley
Mr G.F. Whitehead

**19th – 26th June 1921**
Rev. Dr W.G. Scroggie
Rev. J. Russell Howden
Rev. Dr Charles Inwood
Rev. Gordon Watt
Mr G.F. Whitehead

**19th – 25th June 1922**
Rev. Dr Alex. Smellie
Rev. J. Russell Howden
Rev. Dr F.B. Meyer
Rev. Dr W.Y. Fullerton
Mr G.F. Whitehead

**3rd – 10th June 1923**
Rev. J. Russell Howden
Rev. Dr W.G. Scroggie
Rev. Fred Gibson,
Mr G.F. Whitehead

**22nd – 29th June 1924**
Rev. J. Russell Howden
Rev. Dr Charles Inwood
Rev. Dr A.E. Richardson
Rev. Alexander Frazer
Mr G.F. Whitehead

**21st – 28th June 1925**
Rev. Alexander Frazer
Rev. Dr Swan
Rev. W.W. Martin
Rev. C.H. Lunn

Mr G.F. Whitehead

**20th – 27th June 1926**
Rev. J. Russell Howden
Rev. Alexander Frazer
Rev. Dr W. G. Scroggie
Rev. W.W. Martin
Mr G.F. Whitehead

**19th – 26th June 1927**
Rev. J. Russell Howden
Rev. Alexander Frazer
Rev. Gordon Watt
Rev. W.H. Aldis
Rev. Dr Charles Inwood
Mr G. F. Whitehead

**24th June – 1st July 1928**
Rev. J. Russell Howden
Rev. Alexander Frazer
Rev. Gordon Watt
Rev. H. Earnshaw Smith
Mr G.F. Whitehead

**23rd June – 30th June 1929**
Rev. J. Russell Howden
Rev. Alexander Frazer
Rev. John Macbeath
Rev. W.G. Ovens
Mr G.F. Whitehead
Mr F.J. Scroggie

**22nd – 29th June 1930**
Rev. Alexander Frazer
Rt Rev. Bishop Taylor
Smith
Rev. W. W. Martin

Rev. Dr W. G. Scroggie
Mr G.F. Whitehead

**21st – 28th June 1931**
Rev. W.W. Martin
Rev. John Macbeath
Rev. J.R.S. Wilson
Mr G.F. Whitehead
Mr F. J. Scroggie

**18th – 26th June 1932**
Rev. Alexander Frazer
Mr S.D. Gordon
Rt Rev. Bishop Taylor Smith
Rev. E.W. Mills
Mr G.F. Whitehead

**25th June – 2nd July 1933**
Rev. Alexander Frazer
Rev. Dr W.G. Scroggie
Rev. Canon S.M. Warner
Mr G.F. Whitehead
Mr A. Lindsay Glegg

**24th June – 1st July 1934**
Rev. Alexander Frazer
Mr A. Lindsay Glegg
Rev. J. Russell Howden
Rev. John Macbeath
Mr G.F. Whitehead

**23rd – 30th June 1935**
Rev. Alexander Frazer
Mr A. Lindsay Glegg
Mr G.F. Whitehead
Rev. Colin C. Kerr,
Rev. Dr W.G. Scroggie

**21st – 28th June 1936**
Mr G.F. Whitehead
Rev. Alexander Frazer
Mr A. Lindsay Glegg
Rev. Wm. Grist
Rev. J. Sidlow Baxter

**20th – 27th June 1937**
Rev. H.E. Boultbee
Rev. Alexander Frazer
Mr A. Lindsay Glegg
Rev. J. Macbeath
Rev. Canon S.M. Warner
Mr G.F. Whitehead
Rev. Dr Donald Grey Barnhouse

**19th – 26th June 1938**
Rev. J. Sidlow Baxter
Rev. Dr Donald Davidson
Rev. Colin G. Kerr
Rev. Canon L. Parkinson Hill
Mr G. F. Whitehead

**18th – 25th June 1939**
Rev. Dr Donald Grey Barnhouse
Mr A. Lindsay Glegg
Rev. John Macbeath
Rev. Canon S.M. Warner
Mr G.F. Whitehead
Rev. High E. Boultbee

**23rd – 30th June 1940**
Rev. Geoffrey King
Rev. Canon S.M. Warner
Rev. Chancellor L. Parkinson Hill
Rev. Canon Cooke

**22nd – 29th June 1941**
Mr A. Lindsay Glegg
Rev. Geoffrey King
Rev. Canon Cooke
Rev. Chancellor Parkinson Hill

**21st – 28th June 1942**
Rev. Theo. M. Bamber
Rev. Alexander Frazer
Mr A. Lindsay Glegg
Mr Montague Goodwin
Rev. Martin Parsons

**20th – 27th June 1943**
Rev. J. Sidlow Baxter
Rev. Alexander Frazer
Rev. Martin Parsons
Mr A. Lindsay Glegg
Mr R.E. Laidlaw
Mr T.B. Rees

**18th – 25th June 1944**
Rev. James Dunlop
Rev. Chancellor Parkinson Hill
Rev. W.G.M Martin
Rev. Martin Parsons
Rev. J.B. Wallace

**17th – 24th June 1945**
Rev. H.W. Cragg
Rev. Dr Wm Fitch
Rev. Alexander Frazer
Rev. J. Macbeath
Mr A. Lindsay Glegg
Mr T.B. Rees

*(Source: North of Ireland Keswick Convention Archives)*

# Chapter 10

# What is the Convention all about anyway?

Keswick Conventions have a distinctive spirituality and the Convention at Portstewart is no exception. Our Convention exists to glorify God, through the consecrated lives of believers exposed to the Holy Scriptures, taught, inspired and empowered by the Holy Spirit. Keswick has that strong and specific intention.

Recently we at Portstewart, have adopted the familiar Keswick slogan 'Bringing the Bible Alive' and although that is what we do, we are not merely a 'Bible Week'. Our particular aim is the deepening of spiritual life and the promotion of Scriptural and therefore practical holiness, dependent upon the Holy Spirit. The old adage frequently used is that "a Conference has a subject whereas a Convention has an object". The object we pursue is the glory of God, through His people living consecrated lives in the power of the Holy Spirit. The Convention Committee is always anxious to bring speakers who know God and who are skilled at expounding His Word. Seeking to be true to the Convention's motto we bring speakers from various denominations and indeed from different parts of the world.

Everyone, familiar with Keswick at Portstewart, knows that each day begins with the Prayer Meeting and is followed by the Morning Bible Reading, which is an in-depth study of a Bible book or a Biblical theme. On some days, recently, the Convention has hosted Lunchtime Seminars which are designed to teach and assist believers to be more effective Christian Disciples. The

Evening Meeting, at which the Bible is expounded, is set in a framework of worship using a blend of older and contemporary music and praise. Unlike the Cumbrian Keswick, our Convention had a strong Missionary emphasis from its beginning in 1914. It is of course agreed by all, that by the grace of God, faithful Bible Ministry changes lives and that the call to Service in the power of the Holy Spirit is its natural outflow.

As has been noted, the Keswick Convention was established in 1875 as the product of the Higher Life Movement in Great Britain and it was described in the newspapers under the heading: 'Three days Union Meetings for the Promotion of Practical Holiness'. Reflecting upon the necessity of holiness, the Rev. Dr James Packer wrote in 1992, "... the shift of Christian interest away from the pursuit of holiness to focus on fun and fulfilment, ego massage and techniques for present success, and public issues that carry no challenge to one's personal morals is a fact". Iain Murray, joint founder and Editorial Director of the Banner of Truth, in the 2010 Keswick Lecture commenting upon the decline and marginalization of the church in our day despite much talk about 'spirituality', suggests correctly, that it is a reflection on the quality of the lives of believers. In his lecture *Evangelical Holiness*, he asserts that the emphasis of Keswick is what the church needs today:

> We live in a time, and in a country, where there is massive indifference to Christianity. Unbelief is arrogant. In many parts of the land church buildings are disused and sold, perhaps turned into theatres or public houses. It might therefore be argued that the priorities for Christians today should be reaching the world outside, or defending the truth of the Christian faith. Both are certainly necessary, but the old Keswick priority remains the right one. When Christianity is weak, the fault generally lies not in the world but in the church herself. Let the spiritual health of the church be what it ought to be and there will be no question of her declining impact on the world.

The "old Keswick priority" is 'holiness'. This is a Biblical imperative, and it is expected in both the Old and the New Testaments that the Holy and True God should be worshipped, loved and served by a truthful and holy people.

At the beginning of the Keswick Movement, the founders wanted to establish the fact that what they were teaching about sanctification and the victorious Spirit filled life had an historic precedent. In 1906, the book, *Manual of Keswick*

*Teaching* was published by the Keswick Council. The four contributors were, Handley Moule the Bishop of Durham, Hubert Brooke, Elder Cumming and F.B. Meyer. For Moule, the distinctive feature of Keswick teaching was the discovery of the power of faith, of personal reliance in the matter of purity and liberty within. This according to Moule was not a new doctrine. It was, he believed, Scriptural and, "implied in all the records of the saints". The first Keswick apologists believed that William Romaine and the Puritan, Walter Marshall taught about the possibility of a higher and victorious Christian life. In fact the Rev. Evan Hopkins, the early Keswick theologian and author of *The Law of Liberty in the Spiritual Life* quoted Marshall, who he understood to teach a form of 'sanctification by faith'. At the heart of Keswick was the message of reliance on Christ and personal surrender to Him. Hopkins taught that the believer experiences a "crisis" and this is followed by a "process". Keswick teaching was Bible based, Christ centred, Spirit enabled, practical and mission orientated. This was the movement that inspired both the Rev. Canon Oswald Scott and Mr R.H. Stephens Richardson.

Portstewart borrowed Keswick's method and adopted its traditional sequence of teaching. In 1875 and for some years following, the ministry at Keswick had been testimony orientated. The Bible passages and subjects for the meetings were decided at the Convention. However, a sequence of teaching soon emerged, and this was used at Portstewart Most of the speakers at Portstewart also preached at Keswick and therefore there was a common ministry.

On Monday the subject is 'Sin in the life of the believer'. Keswick takes sin seriously as an insult to the Holy God. As a result of this belief in the seriousness and enslaving nature of sin, Tuesday highlights 'The all sufficient remedy through the redeeming blood of Christ in full Salvation'. The blood of Christ alone can atone and cleanse from sin. On Wednesday 'Surrender and Consecration to Christ', His Word and will is stressed. On Thursday 'The Holy Spirit and the Spirit filled life' is the subject. The consecrated life honours Christ, as it is enabled by the Holy Spirit to glorify God. Then the sequence comes to an end with 'The call to service' on the Friday evening.

The early Keswicks were, and 'Keswick at Portstewart' today is, a kind of spiritual clinic. The attendees come from various denominational backgrounds and for one week they unite with others, in a common desire to meet with God and to do business with Him. The call is to gaze into

God's Word and to see Him in His grace and power. There is an acceptance that differences and strongly held denominational positions are not highlighted. The Convention is a good example of evangelical ecumenicity. This accommodation extends to styles of worship too. The North of Ireland Keswick is not the extension of any denomination and if it ever became so, it would forfeit the right to use the label Keswick.

Originally and until 1919, the Portstewart Convention was held from Monday to Saturday of the last full week of June. In 1920, it met from Monday to Sunday and in 1921, it was held from Sunday to Sunday. In 1922, it reverted to Monday to Sunday but was held thereafter from Sunday to Sunday until 1949 when it was held until 1998, from Saturday until the following Sunday. In 1998 the Convention Committee decided to hold the Convention from Saturday to Friday and this is our practice today. However, in 1923, the Convention was held from 3rd – 10th June because the General Assembly of the Presbyterian Church was commencing on the 20th. In an attempt to reach more people and families the Committee in 2006, changed the date of the Convention to the second full week in July. This change into the N. Ireland traditional holiday period has had the desired effect and has contributed to the recent growth of the Convention.

The tent had to be erected before the first Convention Sunday every year and in 1922, the Convention Committee allowed the Rev. W.P. Nicholson to conduct two evangelistic meetings on Sunday 18th June. The fact that the tent was seated and ready before the Convention began, persuaded the Committee to make use of both weekends. The first weekend was given to preparation for the Keswick sequence of teaching that was to follow from Monday to Friday. The final weekend was a particular challenge because attendees who stayed in guest houses and hotels had to check out on Friday evening or Saturday morning. The Convention leadership wrestled with the challenge of the closing weekend for many years. Eventually, it was taken as an opportunity to develop a particular theme and in 1991, for example, the 'Holiday Weekend' took as its subject 'The Christian Family'. The ministry of the Revs Alastair Morrice and Dr Sandy Roger made that weekend memorable.

The sequence of teaching, outlined above, was most beneficial to attendees who were residential and others who could come to all the meetings. Many people stayed in House Parties organised by the Qua Iboe Mission, the

Egypt General Mission and other Missionary Societies. Portstewart hotels placed adverts in the national press and, along with the local guest houses, catered for the people. Groups came to the Convention from Dublin and from England. In 1938, for example, a sizable group from St. Leonards on Sea, East Sussex came to the Convention. On at least one occasion (1921) the Convention Committee met local guest house owners and hoteliers to discuss a possible reduction in their tariffs. As the Convention became less residential the sequence of Keswick teaching came under some discussion.

# Chapter 11

# Major Convention Personalities (1946-2013)

The leadership of the Convention underwent significant change from 1946 - 2013. Many of the original Committee members died before 1945 and a new team emerged after the War. The leadership was self perpetuating i.e. interested and committed persons were invited to to join the Committee by the Trustees.

Several notable leaders from 1946-2013 have been selected for further comment. Their connections with the business and ecclesiastical life of the North of Ireland resulted in the Convention being trusted and supported among the Protestant people.

Three of the Convention Chairmen since 1946 have been Presbyterian Ministers (Very Rev. Dr James Dunlop, Very Rev. Dr W.M. Craig and the Rev. Dr Joseph Fell); one was a Presbyterian Ruling Elder, (Mr Lawson McDonald) and the other a Quaker, (Mr R. H. Stephens Richardson). From 1946 – 2013, six Honorary Secretaries have been Presbyterians, (Mr R.L. McKeown, Mr James McDonald, Mr Lawson McDonald, Rev. Dr Joseph Fell, Rev. Johnston Lambe and Mr Robin Fairbairn). From 1946 – 2012 one Treasurer was a Quaker (Mr D. McDonagh), two were Anglicans (Mr Walker and Mr Mitchell) and five were Presbyterians (Mr Clyde, Mr T.S. Mooney, Mr W.J. Cairns, Mr J. Petrie, Mr D. Lamb).

# Convention Office Bearers 1946-2013

**Chairman of Convention**

**1917 - 1957**
Mr R.H. Stephens Richardson

**1957 – 1976**
Very Rev. Dr James Dunlop

**1976 - 1991**
Very Rev. Dr William Magee Craig

**1991 - 2004**
Mr J. Lawson McDonald

**2004 - 2013**
Rev. Dr Joseph Fell

**Vice Chairman of Convention**

**1946 – 1950**
Mr A. Lindsay Glegg

**Chairman of Committee**

**1944 - 1976**
Rev. Dr James Dunlop

**1977 - 1983**
Rev. Dr Alan Flavelle

**Joint Honorary Secretaries**

**1944 - 1977**
Mr J. McDonald

**1977 - 1991**
Mr J. McDonald
Mr J. L. McDonald

**1991 - 2004**
Rev. Dr Joseph Fell

**2004 - 2007**
Rev. J. Lambe

**2007 - 2013**
Mr Robin Fairbairn

**Minute Secretary**

**2012**
Rev. Johnston Lambe

**Treasurers**

**1933 - 1950**
Mr Robert Clyde

**1950 - 1965**
Mr George M. Walker

**1965 - 1986**
Mr T.S. Mooney

**1986**
Mr D. McDonagh

**1986 - 1991**
Mr Oswald H.A. Mitchell FRCS

**1991 - 2008**
Mr Williams J. Cairns

**2008 - 2009**
Mr John Petrie

**2009 - 2013**
Mr David Lamb

## Mr Robert Gray Bass:

R.G. Bass joined the Convention Committee on 4th December, 1918. Born in Sheffield, England in 1871, Mr Bass was a lifelong Quaker. *The Irish Evangelistic Society's News Bulletin* of June, 1952 records, "his mother was a recognised minister and had influence over him". In 1891, he came to work in Belfast for Marcus Ward, stationers and printers in Bedford Street. He displayed gifts of leadership, hard work and efficiency and as the same News Bulletin records, "he was destined for other work than selling pens and pencils".

In 1898, he served as a part-time evangelist in Rathfriland, Co. Down alongside a number of Quaker women and Mr William E. Gregory. Their combined efforts were greatly blessed and when civil disorder broke out at the time of the General Election, Mr Bass was able to address both the Unionist and the Nationalist communities and peace was restored. He worked with the YMCA for the duration of the First World War and in 1916, while a Member of their Mission Committee, served amongst 4,000 convalescent Scottish soldiers in Randalstown, Co. Antrim. He was also deeply involved in the 'Catch-my-Pal' Temperance movement.

R.G. Bass was an efficient organiser, a wise Churchman and enjoyed the respect of the evangelical community as an effective evangelist and as Secretary of the Irish Evangelisation Society from 1919. In the 1920s he organised Route Marches throughout the country and witnessed for Christ in many towns and villages. In 1943 – 44, he organised 'Victory Crusades' with Tom B. Rees.

Mr Bass died on 28th January, 1952 and *The Belfast Telegraph* of 16th February, announced that a Memorial Service would be on held on the 17th in the Wellington Hall, Belfast. This event, held under the auspices of the Irish Evangelisation Society, drew 1,400 people. Organised by the Portstewart Convention and the City of Belfast YMCA, the Rev. James Dunlop, Mr R.H. Stephens Richardson and Mr James McDonald took part with Mr David McDonagh, a fellow Quaker; and an Anglican Rector, the Rev. J.C. McLeod; all of whom were members of the Convention Committee. Tributes from the Rev. Dr Alan Redpath and Tom B. Rees were read. It is easy to see how the North of Ireland Keswick was integral to much Christian life in the country in the 1950s.

R.G. Bass was committed to the unity of Christian believers and led an effective Mission to Belfast near the end of his life, at which the Revs Alan Redpath and Geoffrey Lester were the preachers. *The Irish Evangelistic Society's News Bulletin* of June, 1952, records that it was, "the biggest mission the City of Belfast ever had". In its aftermath the City of Belfast Corporation, significantly, offered Mr Bass the use of the Botanic Gardens for four or five Sundays during July and August each year. These meetings ended in the late 1960s with the onset of the N. Ireland Troubles.

R.G. Bass had an international vision and this was worked out, particularly, through the Egypt General Mission and the Bible Society. His ecumenical activities involved, according to the June Bulletin, membership of the Belfast Council of Churches and were a reflection of his personal commitment to Keswick's 'All One in Christ Jesus' motto. At his death, he had served the Convention for 34 years (1918-1952). The Rev. J. Dunlop, at the Memorial Service, said about him, "he belonged to all the Churches and he was wholly Christ's at heart".

At a Convention 'Meeting Point' evening in the 1970s, Mr James McDonald told the audience that Mr Bass was known as 'RGBargie'. He then recounted a memorable story about Mr Bass. One warm Convention evening, Mr Bass, as was his custom, was walking around the tent to ensure that no one disturbed the meeting. A large lady was seen by RGBargie reversing out under the side wall of the tent. Mr Bass was not pleased that anyone should leave early and so he put his shoe on her posterior and gently but firmly pushed her in again. He never met her and she had no idea who had refused her permission to leave!

## The Very Rev. Dr James Dunlop:

In addition to R.G. Bass, another prominent leader in the 1940's and into the 1970s was the Rev. James Dunlop, who joined the General Committee on 5th February 1937. He was converted to Christ under the ministry of the Rev. W. P. Nicholson in his home Congregation of Wellington Street, Ballymena in early 1923. After a distinguished undergraduate career at Trinity College, Dublin from which he graduated with 1st class honours in Mental and Moral Science in 1929 winning the coveted gold medal, his theological studies were taken at Magee Theological College, Londonderry (1929-30), Princeton Seminary, USA (1930-31) and the Presbyterian College, Belfast (1931-32). He was licensed by the Ballymena Presbytery on 25th May, 1932 and, after a period of service in the Church Extension Charge at Greenisland, he was ordained and installed by the Belfast Presbytery on 30th November, 1933 in the Congregation of Oldpark, where he ministered until 1973.

In 1964, he was appointed Moderator of the General Assembly of the Presbyterian Church in Ireland and was awarded the honorary degree Doctor of Divinity by Trinity College, Dublin. The Convention's link with Oldpark was significant for its first Minister the Rev. W. McCoach, had been a member of its Committee from 1918 – 1933; and its Secretary, Mr R.L. McKeown had been an Elder and was Session Clerk when he died in 1942. The Very Rev. Dr A.W. Godfrey Brown wrote in the General Assembly Minutes of 1981:

Dr Dunlop brought to his ministry a keen mind, deep convictions, a warm heart, and a life firmly disciplined and wholly dedicated to the service of his Lord. He was a wise leader, a most attentive pastor, and a preacher of unusual eloquence and power. His gifts in expounding and applying Scripture not only had remarkable results within his own congregation but made him greatly in demand for congregational missions, student addresses and Convention Ministry. On several occasions he was a speaker at the Keswick Convention

There is no doubt that Dr Dunlop's involvement in the North of Ireland Keswick as a Committee member from 1937, and as Chairman of Committee from 1944, gave the movement credibility among a wide spectrum of churchmanship. James Dunlop was an avowed evangelical, but unlike so many, he had a catholicity of heart and mind. He had many friends who did not share his theological opinions. Dr Dunlop acted as de facto Chairman of Convention from 1944 until the death of Mr Richardson on 5th July 1957. He resigned the Chairmanship due to ill health on 20th January, 1976. Dr Dunlop once stated publicly that he considered being Chairman of the Portstewart Convention a greater honour than being Moderator of the General Assembly for one year.

James Dunlop was Chairman of Scripture Union in N. Ireland; the Girl's Crusader Union and a Vice President of the University and Colleges Christian Fellowship. The General Assembly Memorial Minute records,

in the courts of his own denomination he was noted for his wisdom and moderation and for his interest in evangelism and overseas mission. He was joint-Convener of the Foreign Mission from 1956 – 1967 and through his ministry he encouraged a great many men and women to offer for missionary service.

Dr Dunlop had visited N. India for a six months preaching tour in 1957-8 and was involved in some preliminary negotiations which led, after many years, to the formation of the new Church of North India, which was inaugurated at Nagpur on the 29th November 1970. Like Dr F.B. Meyer before him, Dr Dunlop, as Dr J.T. Carson, (cited by Dr Thomas Fitch) said, "yet again we cannot here tell what a fine example he was of the message of 'full salvation' in which he wholeheartedly believed and which he so winsomely proclaimed at Portstewart and Keswick". The Very Rev. Dr W.M. Craig said at the funeral of Dr Dunlop, (cited by Dr Fitch), "for many of us the Portstewart Convention has been and always will be inextricably linked with the name of Dr James Dunlop. He was greatly beloved, too, at the parent Convention in Keswick, and was invited to speak there often". T.S. Mooney, a Treasurer of the Convention, paid Dr Dunlop this great tribute, "he was as ardent an evangelist as Moderator of the General Assembly as when he was a student in his first theological year". Part of the Memorial Tribute to Dr Dunlop by the Convention Committee includes,

> As Chairman of the Convention he was greatly beloved. He had an easy relationship with his audience. Year after year he set the tone for the Convention with his fluent, deeply spiritual opening address. He led the singing with zest and enthusiasm. He welcomed and thanked the speakers with apt and happy phrase. He presided with graciousness and purposefulness. We were all so happy that the Convention was under his skilful and strong control.

The impact of Portstewart upon the church in the North of Ireland and overseas was greatly enhanced through its connection with the Very Rev. Dr James Dunlop. Inspired by his example his son, the Very Rev. Dr H. A. Dunlop served as a Committee member from 1973 to 1993 and as a Joint Youth Convener. His daughter, Mrs Sheila Fell has been involved from the 1970s until the present with various responsibilities.

## Mr James Mc Donald MBE:

James McDonald joined the Committee on 24th June, 1943 when a new era in the Convention's life was about to get underway. R.L. McKeown died on 11th March 1942 and Dr Montgomery, on 17th February 1943, and a new team were urgently required to assume leadership of the Convention. It was led by Dunlop and McDonald into the 1970s. By their close Committee friends they were known simply as, 'the two Jims'.

The Convention Minutes of 7th January, 1944, record the retirement of Mr R.H. Stephens Richardson as Convention Chairman and the appointment of two sub committees to seek a new Chairman and also a new Secretary to replace Mr McKeown. The Minutes of 4th April, 1944, show that the Rev. James Dunlop was appointed Committee Chairman, Mr McDonald was appointed as Secretary and Mr T.S. Mooney was welcomed to the Committee membership. A formidable team had been created. These three Presbyterians ensured that the Biblical and Reformed emphasis in the Convention was maintained. Having said that, they were also committed Keswick men!

James McDonald was ordained as an Elder in Greenisland Presbyterian Church on 13th November, 1949. He and the Rev. James Dunlop became firm friends during the latter's ministry at Greenisland, to which reference has already been made. Some time before, in 1942, James McDonald was appointed the N. Ireland representative for the British and Foreign Bible Society, out of 100 applicants, as Cooney records. Through his work in the Society he had many contacts all over the country and in all the churches. He was a capable Bible teacher and brought his evangelical ecumenicity to the Convention. He was also a great organiser and always careful in writing accurate Minutes and in ensuring that the Convention ran smoothly. The relationship these two men (Dunlop and McDonald) had was simply magnificent. They trusted one another and worked as a great team.

Mr McDonald steered the Convention Committee through some important property matters. He was committed to Keswick and its distinctive spirituality. His wife, son and daughter were involved too, and for many years his daughter, Margaret assisted him with secretarial responsibilities during the week of the Convention. His son, Lawson, followed him as Secretary and was appointed Convention Chairman in 1991. His granddaughter, Janet also served in the office during the Convention week. In other places this might be construed as nepotism. It is not the case, however, as far as the McDonald family were concerned. James McDonald had inspired his family by his teaching and life and they recognised the worth of Keswick as the spiritual reality that had made their husband and father what he was. The Belfast Gazette of 4th January, 1996, records that "Mr James McDonald had been honoured by Her Majesty the Queen in the New Year's Honours list as an Ordinary Member of the Civil Division of the said Most Excellent Order of the British Empire for his services to the British and Foreign Bible Society". He remained a Trustee and a Convention Committee member until his death in 2006.

# Mr A. Lindsay Glegg
## ACGA, AMIEE, JP:

It was agreed to invite Mr A. Lindsay Glegg JP, to act "as Vice Chairman" (of the Convention) "for a term of three years" on 18th September, 1945. Often however, due to his many church and business commitments in Great Britain, he could not be present at the Convention for the whole week. He had been a Speaker at Portstewart in 1933, 1934, 1935, 1936, 1937, 1939, 1942, 1943 and 1945 and went on to preach at the Convention 22 times until 1963. Mr Glegg also preached at some of the many Sunday BBC Radio Broadcasts from the Convention.

The Convention entered the postwar years closely associated with this well-known, popular and respected Christian leader, with his many contacts in the wider British Christian constituency. Mr Glegg had preached at Keswick every year from 1927 to 1939 except 1928. He was a major Christian leader in the UK. The association with Lindsay Glegg brought the Portstewart Convention into an even closer bond with its parent in Keswick, and no doubt, provided a broader perspective to the parochialism of N. Ireland. One of the last things that Dr F.B. Meyer did, before his death, was to write to Mr Glegg, "I have raced you to Heaven, I am just off – see you there".

L. Glegg was of Scottish Presbyterian stock, and after experiencing "assurance of salvation in 1905 at the Keswick Convention", he served as leader of the Down Lodge Hall, Wandsworth, London. Always interested in young people, Lindsay Glegg was involved in the Christian Endeavour movement, serving as National President in 1945-6 when he visited Ireland to address meetings. He was also the National Sunday Union President for two years. His work with young people and his Keswick credentials prepared him to lead the successful Portstewart Convention Youth Meetings during his second visit to the Convention in 1934. Bishop Taylor Smith, a speaker at the Convention in 1930 and 1932, said to him, "concentrate on young people, they will bring you the biggest dividends; you will be able to see in years to come the fruits of your labours". His genuine Christian life, his humanity and sense of humour appealed to the young people.

In 1955, Lindsay Glegg, approached the Keswick Council about the possibility of having meetings during the Convention for the converts of the Billy Graham Crusades in Glasgow and Harringay, London. Price & Randall comment that the Council simply turned the idea down. Determined to do something to encourage the new converts and to point them to full salvation, Glegg and the Rev. Ben Peake initiated 'The Christian Holiday Crusade' at Filey in 1955. According to Glegg himself, the Filey Butlin's Camp had space for nearly 11,000 guests. In 1983 the venue was changed to Skegness and its name eventually became New Horizon. Its demise in 1988 was the major catalyst for the beginning of the New Horizon conference in N. Ireland. Both events, i.e. Keswick at Portstewart and New Horizon were shaped in part, by the personality of Lindsay Glegg and they both arose out of the Keswick Movement. It should be added here, that although both organisations meet around the same time each year and in the same geographic area, there has never been any rivalry between them. L. Glegg's last visit to Portstewart was in 1963. The Very Rev. Dr J T. Carson maintains that Glegg's, "stamp upon the Convention was unmistakable".

## Mr George Montserrat Walker:

Mr G.M. Walker, son Mr M. H. Walker was a member of the Convention Committee from 1942, the Treasurer from 1950-1965 and a Trustee. He carried on the Newtownards Mill after his father died. Mr Walker retired from the Committee due to poor health in 1972. He was a great supporter of many Christian causes including the Inter Varsity Fellowship.

## Mr Thomas Smyth Mooney:

T.S. Mooney joined the Convention Committee in January, 1944. He was a Banker in Londonderry and one of the most, if not, the most influential Ruling Elder in the Presbyterian Church in Ireland for many decades and one of its Trustees. He was ordained by the Presbytery of Derry on 3rd October, 1943 and was appointed as Session Clerk of Kilfennan Congregation in September 1973 and served in that role until his death in 1986.

Mr Mooney was appointed a Trustee of the General Assembly in 1985. 'TS', as he was widely known, was leader of the Londonderry Boys' Crusader Class for 50 years from 2nd November, 1930. T.S. Mooney, in addition to being a much sought after speaker, was also a leader in the Londonderry Christian Workers Union and the founder of the Londonderry Young People's Convention (called 'Keswick in Londonderry' in 1936). 'TS' acted as Chairman of the Londonderry YPC until he retired on 3rd March, 1982. Although it was T.S. Mooney's hope that the Londonderry YPC would be a Keswick style Convention it has no links with the wider Keswick family today, although it still adheres to Biblical ministry. In 2013, it is a Bible Week rather than a Keswick Convention. Mr Mooney was directly involved with the Qua Iboe Mission from 1948 and also with the Londonderry Auxiliary of the Bible Society. He was appointed Treasurer of the Portstewart Convention in 1965 and served for 19 years. Each year at the Convention, Mr Mooney's Treasurer's Report was awaited with anticipation. He always managed, using one or two 'Mooneyisms' to bring the facts and figures in a fresh, humorous and strongly spiritual manner. "TS" was committed to the Keswick message and was a frequent visitor both to Keswick and to the Strathpeffer Convention in Scotland. His Keswick connections were extensive throughout the United Kingdom. It was said of 'TS' that, although his name would not get anyone into Heaven, it would get them into most Christian Fellowships on earth!

In addition, Mr Mooney was widely read in theology and his opinion was sought after by many. While living in the great, historic City of Londonderry, he had contact with successive generations of Divinity students at Magee University and Theological Colleges and his support of the Universities and Colleges Christian Union, was generous. A first year divinity student at Magee in the 1960s confessed that he thought 'TS' was a theological professor!

His contribution into the lives of many generations of church leaders was immense. He died on 24th January, 1986 and over 500 people attended his Funeral in Kilfennan Presbyterian Church, Londonderry. The address at the Funeral was given by the Rev. Dr Alan Flavelle, a fellow Convention Committee member. T.S. Mooney gave the Convention great credence and by his involvement contributed towards its significance.

## Mr David H. McDonagh:

Mr McDonagh was Treasurer for a short time in 1986-1987. Like Mr R.H.S. Richardson he was an evangelical Quaker from near Portadown. It was clear to all who knew him that he was a gentle and Godly man. He was a Director in a successful furniture making company. His love for Christ and the Convention was known to all. Mr McDonagh's sudden death was a severe blow to his family and to all who knew him.

## The Rev. Dr Alan Flavelle:

The much respected Minister of Finaghy Presbyterian Church, Dr Flavelle, was an able theologian and an effective preacher of the Word. He was committed to world mission and served for many years as Chairman of the N. Ireland OMF Committee. He was also deeply committed to the UCCF. The Rev. Flavelle preached at the Keswick Convention in 1981 and at Portstewart in 1969, 1973, 1976 and in 1984. He was appointed Chairman of Committee in 1977 and served in that capacity until 1983. Dr Flavelle was appointed by the Committee to arrange 'Meeting Point', a gathering held for a number of years in the 1970s -1980s, on a few evenings each year after the main Convention

Meeting. He led it with skill and spiritual sensitivity, interviewing Speakers and reiterating the Convention's ministry. The Presbyterian Theological Faculty, Ireland, acknowledged his contribution to the Church worldwide by awarding him the honorary degree of Doctor of Divinity in 1984.

## The Very Rev. Dr John Talbot Carson:

In panoramic photographs of the Convention attendees dating from the mid 1930's, John T. Carson is invariable standing beside his close friend, James Dunlop. They both joined the Committee in 1937. Dr Carson ministered in Wellington Street, Ballymena and then at Trinity Presbyterian Church, Bangor, Co. Down. His knowledge of Keswick and its personalities was prodigious.

John Carson was also a prolific writer, and his *God's River in Spate*, which is an account of the 1859 Ulster Revival and his biography of Frazer of Tain are worth reading. In 1963 he produced the booklet, *Ocean Fulness,* which contains a flavour of the Keswick Message. In 1988 his history of the first 75 years of the Convention, *The River of God is Full*, was published. Dr Carson had a warm personality which was obvious to all who knew him. He was a great encourager of younger Ministers. "JT" as he was affectionately known, conducted the Convention daily Prayer Meeting with wisdom, spirituality and sensitivity for many years.

He was appointed Moderator of the General Assembly in 1969 having received a remarkable 18 out of a possible 21 votes. The Presbyterian Theological Faculty, Ireland conferred the honorary degree of Doctor of Divinity upon him in the same year.

## The Very Rev. Dr William Magee Craig:

Dr W.M. Craig's contribution to the Convention since he became a member of Committee on 28th April, 1950 has simply been immense. He ministered in Ebrington Presbyterian Church, Londonderry and then in 1st Portadown. Dr Craig was in great demand as a Bible teacher and evangelist. He was appointed to be Moderator of the General Assembly of the Presbyterian Church in 1979 and awarded the honorary degree of Doctor of Divinity by the Presbyterian Theological Faculty, Ireland. He had been involved in the campaign to withdraw the Presbyterian Church in Ireland from 'The World Council of Churches'.

While ministering in Londonderry, he introduced many divinity students at the Magee Colleges to Keswick teaching and encouraged them to attend the Convention at Portstewart In 1951 he and his wife acted as host and hostess at one of the Ministers' House Parties, and from 1952 for almost 20 years Dr Craig was in charge of the Open Air Meeting. These were two significant ministries at the Convention. Among his peers, Dr Craig was held in high respect and in 1971, 1974 and 1980 he was invited to be a Speaker at Portstewart. He preached at the parent Keswick Convention in 1970 and 1973. Dr Craig is committed to the Keswick Message and its particular sequence of teaching. He testified to the author of this book that, "Keswick teaching works". He meant that the sequence which exposes sin for what it is, that exalts Christ as the Saviour, that calls for consecration in the power of the Holy Spirit and which results in service, is "a form of sound words" based upon the Holy Scriptures.

He was appointed as Chairman of the Convention as successor to Dr Dunlop in 1976 and served in post for 15 years until 1991. His firm handshake and ready smile were often the first introduction that many people experienced when attending the Convention.

During those years 'The Troubles' were raging and church life in N. Ireland was passing through massive changes. Conservative N. Ireland found change, political or ecclesiastical, hard to manage and the Convention was caught up in it all. Calls for change in praise style and general format of the Convention were coming from some attendees and from a number of Committee members. Meanwhile, the parent Keswick Convention was undergoing similar pressures, and under the guidance of the Rev. Philip Hacking and the Council, Keswick transformed itself while maintaining the Bible, consecration to Christ and service as their essential focus.

Dr Craig was keen to keep the Convention about its main task and on 18th January, 1977 he read a paper, "The Ethos of Keswick" to the Committee. This had been written by Canon A.T. Houghton and had been read to the Keswick Council some time before. Many Portstewart Convention Committee meetings were being held at which the whole structure of the Convention was put under the spotlight, including the youth ministry which was causing particular concern, the two Speaker evening format and the style of the praise.

During the years when Dr Craig was Convention Chairman, attendances at the event remained pretty static. In 1991 the Convention was serving a really important and useful slot in the religious life of N. Ireland and was ready for the next stage of its evolution. Since his resignation, Dr Craig remains a Trustee and a valued member of the Convention Committee.

## Mr James Lawson McDonald:

Mr Lawson McDonald became Chairman in 1991 and during his tenure of office significant changes occurred. Extensive site works were completed in 1998 at a total cost of approximately £79,000. A new bookroom / tent store was built and the orientation of the tent and the seating was altered from a portrait to a landscape style. The 1914 bench seats were replaced by linking chairs and a new platform and backdrop were installed. This all happened during years of uncertainty, while numbers attending were declining and the age profile was rising. At one stage, the future of the Convention was in the balance. However, this work helped to prepare the way for the subsequent years of growth from 2004, because it gave a new image to the jaded one that had slowly evolved. Mr McDonald and the Committee experimented with various music groups and a link with 'Exodus' was established. This link proved to be useful initially but it came to an end in 2004.

In 1995, it was decided to discontinue the two afternoon meetings. An extensive review of the Convention was undertaken in 1997 and the duration of the Convention was changed from Saturday to the following Friday, with one Speaker being responsible for the ministry each evening. This ended the Convention's practice, since 1914, of having two evening Speakers and part of this review endorsed the Keswick scheme of teaching. In 2004, Mr McDonald, anxious not only to publicize the Convention, but to promote it, invited the Rev. Dr Sandy Roger to preach at a number of meetings around the country. He spoke at gatherings in Connor, Co. Antrim; in Cookstown, Co. Tyrone and in the City of Londonderry. In addition, a meeting for Ministers was held in Londonderry.

Following the resignation of Mr McDonald in 2004, the Rev. Dr Joseph Fell acted as both Secretary and Chairman for a short time. Lawson McDonald, in very difficult circumstances, had steered the Convention he loves into calmer waters and made it possible for his successor, to develop and advance its ministry. The Trustees appointed Dr Fell as Chairman, as the Minute of 25th October 2004 records. The Rev. Johnston Lambe, Minister of Montpottinger Presbyterian Church was appointed as Secretary. Dr Fell was given extensive, if not draconian, powers by the Trustees who realized the serious situation the Convention faced. That same Minute records the important decision to change the Convention into the second full week of July.

## Mr William J. Cairns:

Mr Cairns served as Convention Treasurer from 1991-2008. Known to all as "Billy", he was the Accountant in a well-known and successful Estate Agency. He chaired the daily Convention Prayer Meeting for many years. His business acumen was greatly appreciated by the Committee when extensive site works were required in 1997. During the uncertain years, Mr Cairns was a steadying force. He always believed that the main matter before the Committee was the selection of suitable Speakers. Mr Cairns and his wife Zenna, added greatly to the fellowship of the Convention House Party. He was a great encourager of all Biblical ministries and a steadfast supporter of the Convention until he retired in 2012.

## Mr John Petrie:

Mr Petrie served as Treasurer for a short time in 2008-2009. A Presbyterian Elder from Ahoghill, Co. Antrim, he was a keen supporter of the Convention Movement. Like other Convention Treasurers before him, he had worked as a Bank Manager.

# Chapter 12

# The Convention Speakers 1946 – 2013

The Speakers at the Convention 1946 – 2013 were representative of the main line Protestant denominations. The Speakers who were invited most often were: the Rev. G.B. Duncan (Anglican then Presbyterian) 17 times; the Rev. Philip H. Hacking (Anglican and Chairman of the Keswick Council, Cumbria, 1985 to 1993) 13 times; Lindsay Glegg (Independent) 12 times; the Rev. Canon Herbert W. Cragg (Vicar of St. James' Carlisle and subsequently of Christ Church, Beckenham, London) 10 times; the Rev. James Philip (Holyrood Abbey, Church of Scotland, Edinburgh) nine times; the Rev. Dr Raymond Brown (Baptist and former Principal of Spurgeon's College, London) eight times; the Rev. Dr J. Alec Motyer (Anglican and former Principal of Trinity Theological College, Bristol) six times.

The good and Godly Rev. George B. Duncan, formerly of Edinburgh, London and latterly of the Tron Church in Glasgow was a traditional Keswick man. His warm personality and alliteration won him a special place in the hearts of the Portstewart people. GB, as he was known, was a towering figure in every way. His rich voice and obvious love for the Saviour were easily recognised by all who heard him. GB was the preacher at a number of BBC Radio broadcasts from the Convention tent.

The Rev. R.C. Lucus of Bishopsgate, London, who preached at four Portstewart Conventions and the Rev. Eric J. Alexander of Newmills, Ayrshire and the Tron Church of Scotland, Glasgow followed the Keswick sequence of teaching, but were clearer in their presentation and application of it. Mr Alexander became a firm favourite at the five Portstewart Conventions at which he preached. Both of these men, together with the Rev. James Philip of Holyrood Abbey, Church of Scotland, Edinburgh and his brother George of Sandyford Henderson, Glasgow who came to us twice, did much to encourage a more Reformed approach, mixed with passion for God, His Word and for practical holiness.

The Rev. Dr J.G.S.S. Thompson, a notable Scottish Presbyterian Hebraist and Old Testament scholar, was much appreciated by the Portstewart people for his fresh approach to familiar Scriptures. The Rev. Dr Steve Brady, a Baptist and Principal of Moorlands Bible College has been to our Convention on four occasions. Dr Brady, a member of the Keswick Council, brought God's Word to the people with humour, freshness and power.

Throughout the history of the Convention at Portstewart, local preachers have also made their mark. Among them were, the Revs F.C. Gibson, Canon J.W. Cooke, Dr James Dunlop, J.B. Wallace, W.G.M. Martin, Parkinson Hill, Dr William M. Craig, Dr Alan Flavelle, Dr John Girvan, Howard Lewis, John Woodside, Dr Stafford Carson and David Johnston.

In recent years, the Rev. Dr J.A. Motyer with his thorough and intimate knowledge of both Old and New Testaments, mixed with his Irish wit, charm and warmth of personality, did much to convince and to confirm confidence in the total trustworthiness of the Scriptures. Dr Motyer is a prolific author and for many years was the co-editor, with the late Dr J.R.W. Stott, of the 'Bible Speaks Today' series of commentaries published by the Inter Varsity Press. The Rev. Dr Raymond Brown made a massive contribution to Portstewart He has a big heart for people and is a wonderful expositor of God's Word. His many books have inspired countless believers and a number of his commentaries, for example, *The Message of Deuteronomy*, *The Message of Nehemiah* and *The Message of Numbers* were first preached, in part, at the Convention.

The Rev. Philip Hacking the Vicar of Christ Church, Fulwood in Sheffield and former Chairman of 'Reform', helped to reforge the link our Convention has with Keswick. His bouncy style and frequent references to cricket were appealing. As Chairman of the Keswick Council, he oversaw the transformation of Keswick and inspired some of the Portstewart Committee to look to the future while appreciating the best of the past.

The Rev. Alastair Morrice, who has been with us on five occasions, brought both a passion for Christ and a clear exposition of God's Word coloured by his experience in Asia. He and the Rev. Dr Liam Goligher will be joining the Speakers Team in 2013. Dr Goligher, Minister of 10th Presbyterian, Philadelphia and formerly of Kirkintullaght Baptist Church and Duke Street Church, Richmond has been at Portstewart on four previous occasions. In 2007 he wrote a book in defence of the Biblical doctrine of Penal Substitution entitled, *The Jesus Gospel*. They will be joined, in 2013, by the Rev. Jonathan Lamb, former Chairman of the Keswick Council and currently Director of Langham Preaching with the Langham Partnership.

In July 1955, the Rev. Dr James Packer, who had never been to the Keswick Convention, wrote an article in *The Evangelical Quarterly* entitled *Keswick and the Reformed Doctrine of Sanctification*. He popularized its contents in his 1984 Inter Varsity Press publication, *Keep in Step with the Spirit* and then again in 1988, through *Christianity Today*. Dr Packer accused Keswick of being "Pelagian through and through". He based his information about Keswick upon S. Barabas's book, *So Great Salvation*. Dr Packer has written several important books about the subject of 'holiness'. His problem with 'old Keswick' was that, in his opinion, too much emphasis was put upon personal surrender and trust so that it was almost a 'let go and let God' route to sanctification. Long before Packer, Professor B.B. Warfield in the 1930s had made similar criticisms of Dr Asa Mahan, Oberlin Theology, and the Higher Life and Victorious Life Movements of his day.

It is generally acknowledged however, that the Keswick Convention of 1965, at which the late Rev. Dr J.R.W. Stott was responsible for the Bible Readings, was a significant one. It was a kind of watershed. John Stott, who sadly never preached at Portstewart, took Romans Chapters 6-8 as the Scripture for his exposition. Subsequently, the talks were published by the Inter Varsity Press under the title *Men made New*. Dr Stott gave a masterly account of the chapters and offered Keswick an alternative interpretation to some of the verses. The author of this book, as a young university undergraduate, was present at the 1965 Keswick and remembers something of the debate that was caused by this. In 1967, Dr Alan Redpath fired a salvo at Stott's position but to no avail. 'Portstewart', because it shared many Speakers with Keswick, generally followed Keswick's line. However a new generation of preachers was appearing.

## Speakers at the North of Ireland Keswick Convention 1946-2013

**23rd – 30th June 1946**
Rev. J. Sidlow Baxter
Rev. Dr Wm. Fitch
Rev. H. W. Cragg
Rev. Dr Donald
Barnhouse
Mr A. Lindsay Glegg

**22nd – 29th June 1947**
Rev. J. Sidlow Baxter
Rev. Alexander Frazer
Rev. G.B. Duncan
Rev. William Still
Mr A. Lindsay Glegg
Mr J. Oswald Sanders

**20th – 27th June 1948**
Rev. T.C. Hammond
Rev. Prof. R.A. Finlayson
Rev. G. B. Duncan
Rev. Alan Redpath
Mr A. Lindsay Glegg

**18th – 26th June 1949**
Rev. Alexander Frazer
Rev. Wm Leathern
Rev. H. W. Cragg
Rev. Dr Thomas Fitch
Rev. Geoffrey R. King
Rev Prof. R.A. Finlayson

**17th - 25th June 1950**
Rev. G. B. Duncan
Rev. D. Leitch
Rev. Canon Marcus
Loane
Rev. J. MacBeath
Mr David Tryon

**16th – 24th June 1951**
Rev. H. W. Cragg
Rev. C. M. Hilton Day
Rev. Dr Wm. Fitch
Rev. H. R. Harding Wood
Mr A. Lindsay Glegg

**21st – 29th June 1952**
Rev. J. Sidlow Baxter
Rev. G. B. Duncan
Rev. Ian M. MacRury
Mr Stephen F. Olford
Mr A. Lindsay Glegg

**20th - 28th June 1953**
Rev. Duncan Campbell
Rev. Geoffrey R. King
Rev. J.G.S.S. Thompson
Rev. G.R. Harding Wood
Mr A. Lindsay Glegg

**19th – 27th June 1954**
Rev. H. W. Cragg
Rev. G. B. Duncan
Rev. Godfrey C.
Robinson
Rev. Dr J.G.S.S.
Thompson
Mr A. Lindsay Glegg

**18th – 26th June 1955**
Rev. H. W. Cragg
Rev. James Dunlop
Rev. Dr Herbert Lockyer
Rev. Dr J.G.S.S.
Thompson
Mr A. Lindsay Glegg

**16th - 24th June 1956**
Rev. G. B. Duncan
Rev. Duncan Leitch
Rev. Andrew MacBeath
Rev. A.W. Rainsbury
Rev. George Thomas
Mr A. Lindsay Glegg

**22nd – 30th June 1957**
Rev. Dr Wm. Fitch
Rev. Wm. Leathem
Rev. James Philip
Rev. A. Redpath
Rev. A. Skevington Wood
Mr T.B. Rees

**21st – 29th June 1958**
Rev. H. W. Cragg
Rev. Duncan Leitch
Rev. A. W. Rainsbury
Rev. Dr Paul S. Rees
Mr A. Lindsay Glegg

**18th – 26th June 1960**
Rev. H. W. Cragg
Rev. Gerald B Griffiths
Rev. Duncan Leitch
Rev. James Philip
Rev. John B. Taylor

**17th - 25th June 1961**
Rev. John Bird
Rev. G. B. Duncan
Rev. J. Glyn Owen
Rev. A.W Rainsbury
Rev. Dr Paul S. Rees

**16th – 24th June 1962**
Rev. Eric J. Alexander
Rev. H. W. Cragg

Rev. D. Leitch
Mr A. Lindsay Glegg
Dr Howard W. Ferrin

**15th – 23st June 1963**
Rev. G. B. Duncan
Rev. J. Graham Miller
Rev. Dr Paul S. Rees
Rev. K.F.W. Prior
Rev. Geoffrey R. King
Mr A. Lindsay Glegg

**20th – 28th June 1964**
Rev. John Bird
Rev. D.E.D. Churchman
Rev. Philip H. Hacking
Rev. J. Glyn Owen
Rev. Dr J.G.S.S. Thompson

**19th – 27th June 1965**
Rev. Peter H. Barber
Rev. G. B. Duncan
Rev. A.W. Rainsbury
Rev. Dr Paul S. Rees
Rev. Peter E. Street

**18th – 26th June 1966**
Rev. D. Leitch
Rev. J.A. Motyer
Rev. J. Glyn Owen
Rev. A. Redpath
Mr D. Stuart Briscoe

**17th – 25th June 1967**
Rev. H. W. Cragg
Rev. G. B. Duncan
Rev. David McKee
Rev. Philip H. Hacking
Dr Harold B. Kuhn
Dr William Cuthbertson

**22nd – 30th June 1968**
Rev. E. J. Alexander
Rev. D.E.D. Churchman
Rev. Harold W. Fife
Rev. J. Glyn Owen
Rev. K.F.W. Prior

**21st - 29th June 1969**
Rev. E.J. Alexander
Rev. Richard T. Bewes
Rev. John L. Bird
Rev. Alan Flavelle
Rev. Dr A. Skevington Wood

**20th – 28th June 1970**
Rev. G. B. Duncan
Rev. Philip Hacking
Rev. James Philip
Rev. Dr Paul S. Rees
Rev. Dr J.G.S.S. Thompson
Mr Alan G. Nute

**19th - 27th June 1971**
Rev. Alan Redpath
Rev Canon H.W. Cragg
Rev. Duncan Leitch
Rev. K.F.W. Prior
Rev. W.M. Craig
Dr William Cuthbertson

**17th – 25th June 1972**
Rev. J. Sidlow Baxter
Rev. James Philip
Rev. J. Glyn Owen
Rev. Dr Raymond Brown
Rev. Philip H. Hacking

**16th – 24th June 1973**
Rev. G. B. Duncan
Rev. Dr Paul S. Rees

Rev. Alan Flavelle
Rev. Tom Houston
Rev. Gordon Bridger

**15th – 23rd June 1974**
Rev. Philip H. Hacking
Rev. Dick Lucas
Rev. W.M. Craig
Rev. John L. Bird
Capt. Stephen Anderson

**21st – 29th June 1975**
Rev. Dr Paul S. Rees
Rev. Stephen Olford
Rev. D.N. Carr
Rev. Gordon Bridger
Rev. Eric J. Alexander

**10th – 27th June 1976**
Rev. G. B. Duncan
Rev. Francis W. Dixon
Rev. Harry Sutton
Rev. Alan Flavelle
Rev. George Philip

**18th – 26th June 1977**
Rev. K.F.W. Prior
Rev. Sinclair B. Ferguson
Rev. James Philip
Rev Paul Tucker
Rev. Philip H. Hacking

**17th – 25th June 1978**
Rev. Canon H.W. Cragg
Rev. E.J. Alexander
Rev. Harry Kilbride
Rev. Eric Gosden
Rev. Dick Lucas

**6th – 24th June 1979**
Rev. G. B. Duncan
Rev. Dr Raymond Brown
Rev. J. Glyn Owen

Rev. Keith A. A. Weston
Rev. W.C. Filby

**21st – 29th June 1980**
Rev. Philip H. Hacking
Rev. David C. Searle
Rev. Sinclair B. Ferguson
Rev. Dick Lucas
Rev. W.M. Craig

**20th – 28th June 1981**
Rev. James Philip
Rev. Martin A.W. Allen
Rev. Keith A. A. Weston
Rev. Dr J.G.S.S.
Thompson
Rev. Derek Prime

**19th - 27th June 1982**
Rev. Philip H. Hacking
Rev. Dr Raymond Brown
Rev. David C. Searle
Rev. G. B. Duncan
Rev. John Girvan

**18th – 26th June 1983**
Rev. David J. Jackman
Rev. Dick Lucas
Rev. K.F.W. Prior
Rev. Bruce Milne
Rev. Martin A. W. Allen

**16th – 24th June 1984**
Rev. Philip H. Hacking
Rev. Keith A.A. Weston
Rev. Alan Flavelle
Rev. Mariano Di Gangi
Rev. Dick Dowsett

**15th – 23rd June 1985**
Rev. Alan Neech
Rev. Derek Prime
Rev. James Philip

Rev. Hugh Morgan
Rev. David Smith

**21st – 29th June 1986**
Rev. Dr J.G.S.S.
Thompson
Rev. William G. Hughes
Rev. G. B. Duncan
Rev. Martin A.W. Allen
Rev. Alastair Begg

**20th - 28th June 1987**
Rev. James Philip
Rev. Robert G.M. Amess
Rev. K.F.W. Prior
Rev. A.M. Roger
Rev. Alistair Morrice

**18th – 26th June 1988**
Rev. Philip H. Hacking
Rev. G. B. Duncan
Rev. Dr Raymond Brown
Rev. Derek Prime
Rev. David Smith

**17th -25th June 1989**
Rev Peter Barber
Rev. K.F.W. Prior
Rev. Sandy Roger
Rev. Prof. J. D. MacMillan
Rev. Martin A. W. Allen

**16th – 24th June 1990**
Rev. J.A. Motyer
Rev. James Philip
Rev. Dennis Lennon
Rev. David J. Jackman
Rev. Martin Goldsmith

**22nd - 30th June 1991**
Rev. Robert G.M. Amess
Rev. Dr Raymond Brown
Rev. Alastair Morrice

Rev. A. M, Roger
Rev. G. B. Duncan

**20th – 28th June 1992**
Rev. J.A. Motyer
Rev. Canon Gordon
Bridger
Rev. Derek Prime
Rev. Alistair Begg
Rev. Roy Clements

**19th – 27th June 1992**
Rev. Philip H. Hacking
Rev. John Woodside
Rev. David Ellis
Rev. Michael Wilcock
Rev. Alastair Morrice

**25th June – 3rd July
1994**
Rev. Dr Raymond Brown
Rev. Dr Steve Motyer
Rev. Colin Sinclair
Rev. Dr Steve Brady
Rev. Martin A. W. Allen

**24th June - 2nd July
1995**
Rev. George Philip
Rev. Robert Kee
Rev. Dr John Davis
Rev. Ian Hamilton
Rev. Dr A.M. Roger

**22nd – 30th June 1996**
Rev. Canon Keith A.A.
Weston
Rev. Mark Ashton
Rev. Howard Lewis
Rev. Liam Goligher

**21st – 29th June 1997**
Rev. J.A. Motyer

Rev. Robert Kee
Rev. Alastair Morrice
Rev. Hugh Watt

**20th - 26th June 1998**
Rev. Robert Amess
Rev. Philip H. Hacking
Rev. Colin Sinclair

**19th – 25th June 1999**
Rev. Dr Andrew
Magowan
Rev. Dr J.A. Motyer
Rev. Hugh Palmer

**24th – 30th June 2000**
Rev. Dr Raymond Brown
Rev. Liam Goligher
Rev. Dr Derek Tidball

**23rd - 29th June 2001**
Rev. Robert Amess
Rev. Robert Kee
Rev. Dr J.A. Motyer

**22nd – 28th June 2002**
Rev. Mark Ashton
Rev. Dr Raymond Brown
Rev. Dominic Smart

**21st – 27th June 2003**
Rev. Philip H. Hacking
Rev. Colin Sinclair
Rev. Paul Williams

**19th - 25th June 2004**
Rev. Liam Goligher
Rev. Philip Hair
Rev. Robert Kee

**18th- 24th June 2005**
Rev. Dr Steve Brady
Rev. Canon Robert Kee
Rev. A.M. Roger

**8th – 14th July 2006**
Rev. David Johnston
Rev. Charles Price

**7th – 13th July 2007**
Rev. Stafford Carson
Rev. Liam Goligher
Rev. Peter Lewis

**12th – 18th July 2008**
Rev. Dr Steve Brady
Rev. John Woodside
Rev. Dr Chris Wright

**11th – 17th July 2009**
Rev. Bob Flayhart
Rev. Alastair Morrice

**10th – 16th July 2010**
Rev. Craig Dyer
Rev. Dr Derek Thomas
Rev. Paul Williams

**9th – 15th July 2011**
Rev. Edwin Ewart
Rev. David Johnston
Very Rev. Dean Robert
Kee

**13th – 20th July 2012**
Rev. David Scott
Rev. Dr Chris Wright
Rev. Dr Steve Brady

**13th-19th July 2013**
Rev. Dr Liam Goligher
Rev. Alastair Morrice
Rev. Jonathan Lamb

*Source: The North
of Ireland Keswick
Convention Archives,
(1:1914-1989;
2:1990-2013)*

*Qua Iboe Mission (now Mission Africa) House Party at the Windsor Hotel on the Promenade in 1936.*

*Mr R.H. Stephens Richardson, Chairman of Convention 1917-1957.*

*Bookroom presented by Mr R.H.S. Richardson in memory of his wife Mrs Richardson at the 1939 Convention.*

*Some women at the Qua Iboe Mission House Party in 1942.*

*Members of the Cairn Moore House Party at the 1945 Convention.*

*The Rev. James Dunlop – Chairman of Committee 1944-1958 and of Convention 1957-1976.*

The late 1940's Convention Committee at Portstewart 1st left in front row is Mr R.G. Bass then Dean Cooke, Mr R. Clyde, Mr R.H. Stephens Richardson, J. Dunlop and Mr J. McDonald. T.S. Mooney is 2nd from the right in the second row.

The Rev. George B. Duncan (3rd from left) – with Lindsay Glegg (left) and friends in House Party in 1952. Both men were popular Speakers till the mid 1960s

Convention House Party and guests at the Windsor Hotel in 1990. Front row from left: Mr J. McDonald (Joint Secretary), Rev Dennis Lennon Mrs Sheila Fell, Mrs Jessie McDonald, Mr J. McDonald (Joint Secretary), and the Very Rev. Dr W.M. Craig (Chairman). 2nd row: Revs Dr J.A. Motyer, Martin Goldsmith. David Temple, Mrs Maud Crag, Rev James Philip. Back row: Revs Joseph Fell, Norman Brown, Mr W.J. Cairns and Rev. David Jackman.

*The Revs Alastair Morrice, Philip Hacking and David Wilcock on the Platform at the 1993 Convention.*

*The Rev. Norman Brown leads the praise supported by Chairman, Secretary and the full team of Speakers at the 1994 Convention.*

*The Revs George Philip, Canon Robert Key, Ian Hamilton, Dr John Davis, Dr Sandy Roger at the 1994 Convention.*

*The Rev Philip Hacking in 'full flight' at the 1998 Convention*

*Revs Dean R. Key, Hugh Watt, Alastair Morrice and Dr J.A. Motyer in 'Caste Erin' during the 1997 Convention.*

# Chapter 13

# The Convention's Missionary Emphasis

From the very beginning, the North of Ireland Keswick Convention had a Missionary emphasis. The Convention leaders believed in the truth of 'extra Ecclesiam nulla sulus', i.e. there is no salvation outside the Church. At the very first Convention, Mr R.L. McKeown organised the Missionary Meeting and the Minutes of 8th December, 1914, record the amount of the Missionary offering taken on Thursday 25th June, 1914 as being £25.6.4p. This amount was divided among the missionary societies represented, namely the Church Missionary Society, the Irish Presbyterian Church, Qua Iboe and the Egypt General Mission. In addition, some contributions were specifically earmarked to particular societies; 15 shillings (75 new pence) for the London Jews Society; 10 shillings (50 new pence) for the Egypt General Mission and 11 shillings (55 new pence) for Qua Iboe, "making a total of £27.2.4 pence for missionary purposes". The policy of distributing the missionary offering among the societies represented at the Missionary Meeting was continued in 1916 and confirmed in 1923:

> It was agreed as in previous years to give missionaries belonging to any of the accredited societies who are attending the Convention an opportunity of speaking at the [Missionary] meeting, and to explain on the Missionary Offering envelopes that any money not allocated by the donors should be divided equally among the societies represented by speakers.

The Convention Committee, aware that mission begins at home, discussed the possibility in 1922, of having an additional Missionary Meeting focusing on Home Mission.

At the same Committee Meeting it was decided, "if possible to invite all the missionaries present next year to Tea". This Missionary Reception was to continue until the late 1990s. In 1931 approximately 50 were present at the Missionary Tea. The amount of the Missionary Offering in 1923, as recorded in the Minute of 26th June, was, "£204 of which about £170 was allocated by the donors". The Missionary Policy was refined and updated in 1924 when it was decided, "that as far as possible only Missionaries attending the Convention should speak at the Missionary Meeting". This practice was confirmed on 5th May 1925. Clearly the Convention Committee was anxious that no Society would merely use the Convention to extract funding. Missionary Societies, it seems, were pushing the boundaries of the policy and it was further refined, "that only Missionaries attending the Convention, at least from the middle of the week should take part in the Missionary Meeting". At the same Committee Meeting it was agreed "to wire the Mission to Lepers regretting that an opportunity could not be given to a representative coming on Saturday". At this stage in its life, the Convention was a coveted platform for Missionary Societies and reveals the position it enjoyed among the Protestant Community in the North of Ireland.

A significant development in the Convention's Missionary strategy was to consider assisting with training of Missionary candidates. The Minutes of 31st August ,1923, record, "a number of young people in the North of Ireland recently converted are desirous of going abroad and it was felt that something should be done to advise and encourage them and it was agreed if possible to convene a meeting of those interested". However there is no further record of anything being done about this. To further the cause of Mission among the young people it was agreed on 15th April, 1930, that "the youth meetings would be of a missionary nature".

It is clear from the Minutes of the Convention Committee of 4th April, 1928, that although no names of Missionaries sharing at the Missionary Meeting are given in some years, the Meeting was held on the closing Saturday of the Convention. It was changed to the Friday morning in 1952 because fewer missionaries were attending and the declining lack of support for the Saturday morning Meeting. On 27th January, 1975, it was decided to have fewer reports and a shorter address by one of the Convention Speakers. Sadly, this had the effect of changing the import of the Keswick sequence of Teaching, for the Call to Service is the theme for Friday evening. Originally the Missionary Meeting followed the call to service!

The number of missionaries attending the Convention seems to mirror the fortunes of the Convention. Fewer missionaries were attending in the 1970s and some serious consideration was given to how this should be addressed. The Committee on 18th January, 1975, considered using the Guysmere Youth Centre, Castlerock for a Missionary House Party. At the same meeting they heard a report that Keswick had been contacted about their 'Missionary Hospitality Fund'. This allowed Missionaries to attend the whole Convention and receive part of their accommodation expenses. Dr Bill Holley, a Committee member, was deputed to administer this Fund which was established on 18th January, 1977.

Contact was maintained throughout the 1970s until 2013 with the 'Missionary Secretaries Fellowship', so that the Convention could maximise the impact of the Ministry to Missionaries and keep the Missionary mandate before the Convention. At the Committee meeting held on 5th December 1983, the Rev. Bill Leech, a Committee member and the General Secretary of the Qua Iboe Mission, brought several innovative ideas to the members. Rather than majoring on Societies, he thought that regions could be focused upon and that a marquee could be hired to house a significant Missionary Exhibition.

However in 1987, the number of missionaries attending was fewer than usual and this caused major concern. In 1989 the Missionary Reception was moved to Tuesday afternoon. Further good ideas were forthcoming and in 1992 the use of 'The Christian Service Centre' for counselling those who felt the call of God upon their lives was considered. This was a genuine attempt to be proactive in assisting people of all ages to follow through on the Keswick message of consecration and subsequent service. In 1994, another consideration, which was not implemented sadly, was to invite the 'fruit of mission' to the Convention, i.e. someone who was the product of missionary endeavour. This would have inspired missionary interest and exposed Irish Christians to Bible ministry from another culture and context.

In the early 1990s, the North of Ireland Keswick Convention had lost its former standing as 'the place to be' for local Christian people and this was reflected in the gradual décline of Missionaries in attendance at the event. In 1997, the Missionary Secretary, Dr Tom Geddis (now serving Christ in Brazil) indicated that he was having difficulties obtaining Missionaries to address the Missionary Meeting. In 1998 the Missionary Meeting was discontinued and was replaced by regular Mission input at the evening Convention meetings and by a manned Missionary exhibition in the main marquee. Again in 2005, the 'fruit of mission' idea was floated but not taken up. Nowadays the Missionary input is brought through the Missionary Exhibition and by a highlighted Mission or Agency having a spot at one or two evening meetings. In 2010 and 2011 that Agency was, 'The International Fellowship of Evangelical Students'. In 2012 it was 'The Langham Partnership'. The Missionary Offering is given to the selected Agency. Recently, at a Speakers and Planning sub Committee Meeting, the idea of bringing personnel from overseas, was again suggested as having potential.

By all of this activity, the Great Commission given by the Risen Saviour has been set before the Convention. In addition, many Missionaries have come to the Convention and have been encouraged by the ministry to return to their spheres of service with renewed vigour. Many Convention Ministry CDs and DVDs have been sent to missionaries throughout the world. Although no Keswick Convention, anywhere, is a missionary conference, the fact is that thousands of people have been challenged and many have responded to the call to go and "make disciples of all nations".

I have researched a number of people who were called at Portstewart and I give a summary of their stories.

## Dr Bill Holley:

On Thursday 26th June, 1947, Bill Holley heard God's Call to Missionary service in Nigeria. Corbett relates the incident,

> The annual Portstewart Convention has been the scene of many a spiritual battle and life changing experience. On the last Thursday in June 1947, Bill Holley was among a great crowd in the big tent, listening to a notable and much loved speaker, Canon Herbert W. Cragg. 'Speak to the children of Israel that they go forward', came the Word of God, and, deep within, came a prompting of the Holy Spirit – 'to Qua Iboe'. Bill had been sitting beside his future father-in-law. As they came out of the tent Bill surprised him by announcing, "We're going to Qua Iboe!"

This same text had been used to call Amy Carmichael years before. The speakers in 1947 were, Rev. J. Sidlow Baxter, who preached at the morning Bible Readings, the Revs Herbert W. Cragg, George B. Duncan, William Still, Alexander Frazer and the Vice Chairman, Mr Lindsay Glegg, who were responsible for the other meetings. J. Oswald Sanders was also in the Convention 'Cairn Moore' House Party.

Canon H. W. Cragg was the Church of England Vicar of St. James', Carlisle and it was his third visit to the Convention. The Convention was in its postwar heyday and the tent had just been enlarged to seat 2,500 people. The Chairman of the Convention, Mr R.H. Stephens Richardson in his introductory note in the official programme wrote: "Let us therefore come up to the great tent of meeting with earnest prayer and preparedness of heart, seeking to know only the will of the Lord and the Word He would say to us; and we shall assuredly not be sent away disappointed". That prayer was answered in Bill Holley's life and he was to become a distinguished missionary doctor in Nigeria.

William Martin Holley was born in Coleraine, Co. Londonderry, on 2nd June, 1917. His father was a building contractor and Bill had three brothers and one sister. While a pupil at Coleraine Academical Institution, Bill played for the 1st XV rugby team and, after working in the building industry for a short time, decided to study medicine at the Queen's University of Belfast where he a became Football Blue. Bill's life at University was barren as he sought for reality and meaning in socially acceptable drugs but a crisis came in 1940. His mother was seriously ill, a close friend died and the Nazi Blitz of Belfast was underway when God spoke to Him as he watched the Nazi flares fall on Belfast from the roof of the City Hospital. With a fellow student he knelt, repeated the words of John 3:16 – and gave his life to Christ.

Bill's spiritual walk was erratic at first and he enlisted in the Royal Navy because he liked the uniform, and the alcohol and tobacco would be duty free. A friend pointed him to John 1:12 and on 10th August, 1942, Bill Holley received assurance of his salvation. Eventually he joined HMS Test and two and a half years of his war service were spent in the Springtown Naval base, near Capetown.

On Easter Monday 1946, while speaking at the Faith Mission's Bangor Convention, he met a former nurse, a student at Ridgelands Bible College. She was Marion Jenks from Belfast and, after their engagement, Bill had his life changing experience at the Portstewart Convention. He wanted "to do pioneer medical work" and they were both interviewed by the Qua Iboe Council on 2nd October, 1947. They were accepted and in January 1950 sailed for Nigeria. Bill and Marion served leprosy patients in the Etinan and Igala Hospitals before moving to Ochadamu in 1951. Not only did Bill care for the physical needs of the patients, but he was also an able preacher and was responsible under God for the conversion of many people. In 1953, Ochadamu had 530 patients and Dr Holley saw the need for properly built brick buildings. On one of his home deputations a young carpenter and his wife, Mervyn and Florence Crooks, were called through his ministry and they joined Bill in the construction of the new hospital.

Mervyn Crooks eventually became a Missioner in the Londonderry Presbyterian City Mission from 1st October, 1964 – 30th August, 1966. The Mission had three Halls, Marlborough Hall, Bennett Street Hall and Rosemont Hall and offered a wide range of ministry including Sunday Schools, Bible Classes, Men's and Women's Meetings as well as Sunday Services. Mervyn then studied for, and gained a Bachelor of Divinity degree from the Presbyterian Theological Faculty, Ireland and was ordained into the ministry of the Presbyterian Church in Ireland, serving as ordained Assistant Minister at Glengormely (1968 – 1970), then as Minister of Newmills and Carland (1970 – 1975). Portrush (1975 – 1983) and in Newtownstewart and Gortin (1983 – 1994).

The Rev. Mervyn Crook's son is the Rev. Dr Rodger M. Crooks, Minister of Belvoir Park Presbyterian Church, in Belfast and is the author of several important theological books. He has been Convener of some significant General Assembly Committees. The ministry of the Rev. Mervyn and Mrs Crooks and their family have had a God honouring impact on the Church in Ireland and overseas.

Bill Holley, when home on deputation in 1953, preached in Portstewart Town Hall and Cecil his youngest brother was present. God brought Cecil Holley "under a heavy dose of conviction" and he was converted. In 1955 Cecil was to be ordained by the East Belfast Presbytery to the Eldership of the Presbyterian Church in Ireland in Ravenhill Congregation, Belfast where the Rev. John Ross, a member of the 1914 Convention Committee had been the founder Minister. Cecil, a Banker, became a faithful Youth Worker and mentor to generations of young people and a member of the Belfast Young People's

Convention Committee. He also served as the Ravenhill Session Clerk and as a leader in the Young People's Christian Endeavour Society from 1953, until it became the 'Young Adults' in 1969.

The Holleys left Nigeria on 12th October, 1961, and Corbett writes, "as news leaked out that the doctor might not be returning from furlough there was a great lamentation at Ochadamu and throughout Igala".

Returning to N. Ireland, Dr Holley served as Senior Medical Officer in the Route Hospital, Ballymoney and then became a partner in Dr Burn's practice in Coleraine. Bill was invited to join the Committee of the Portstewart Convention on 11th November 1966. As a member, he encouraged missionary endeavour and supervised the 'Missionary Hospitality Fund'. Dr W.M. Craig, the Convention Chairman (cited by Corbett) describing Dr Holley's great contribution to the Convention said,

> ... the consistent fragrance and influence of his life, embodying the truths that were proclaimed from the platform. His smile was genuine, his eyes were sincere, his handshake was firm and his countenance radiated the joy of the Lord with whom He walked.

On 9th November 1970, Bill Holley met Arthur Williams, a man with a dreadful alcohol addiction. Bill, before he treated Arthur, told him that he needed Christ and after prayer Arthur gave his life to Jesus. Arthur eventually studied theology at Cliff College, Derbyshire after which he became Pastor of Findlay Memorial Church in Glasgow. According to Corbett, the Congregation had a close relationship with the Qua Iboe Mission, presenting a shield each year to the best Sunday School in the Qua Iboe Church. He served in Glasgow for six years, leading many drug addicts to the Saviour, before returning to N. Ireland to found 'The Stauros Foundation'. 'Stauros' is the Greek word for Cross and its ministry is predicated on the belief that addicts can find sobriety through the work of Christ on the Cross. The Stauros Foundation's work spread to Scotland and to England and is still greatly used by God.

Dr Holley moved to be Senior Medical Officer at Magilligan Prison in Co. Londonderry in 1978, when the N. Ireland 'Troubles' were at their height and many Loyalist and Republican prisoners were being held there. He identified with the newly formed 'Prison Fellowship' and worked with the four Prison Chaplains to offer the holistic Christian way of life to all. Both sides of the Ulster divide attended the Bible studies he organised. According to James McIlroy (cited by Corbett):

After a few initial restraints, republicans and loyalists shared their hymn sheets and sang heartily together. They listened attentively to the short challenging talks and, as time progressed, we saw friendships formed where there was enmity before.

It has been attested often, that the seeds of hope in N. Ireland were sown in the prisons. For example, Michael, a Marxist and an Irish National Liberation Army Volunteer was converted; as was Sean, a former Republican who had been on hunger strike for 56 days in 1981. A letter from Sean (cited in Corbett) in which he says that he left the INLA, and that Jesus "has brought me freedom, freedom from hatred, freedom from selfishness, freedom from bitterness and lust – freedom of spirit. Although I am still bound physically behind locked doors and gates, I am free, for freedom of mind is freedom indeed".

On 20th May 1984, Bill was diagnosed as suffering from Motor Neurone Disease and died on 10th June 1985. Near the end of his life, when the disease had gripped his body, he typed onto a computer screen "all the days of my life are recorded in Thy book" – and again – "no fears just family tears". Liam, a converted terrorist while on parole called to see the Holleys and commented that Bill's faith,

> hadn't been shaken one iota by the disease he was suffering from. His family hadn't been shaken. His wife, Marion was remarkable, and his son and daughters. That strengthened my faith and it made me determined to have a relationship with God that could sustain me through something as horrible as they had to go through.

As a memorial to Dr Bill Holley, the Qua Iboe Church in 1990, named the Ochadamu Medical Centre, the Holley Memorial Hospital. Such was the contribution for Christ in Ireland and to the world church by a man called at the Portstewart Convention.

## Oswald H.A. Mitchell MB, FRCS:

Oswald Mitchell, a Belfast boy, was born in 1926 into an Anglican family and belonged to St. Paul's Parish Church, York Street. His parents were devout Christians with a genuine interest in worldwide missionary endeavour. They thought so highly of their Rector, the Rev. Canon Oswald W. Scott that they gave their son, the Rector's Christian name. In his formative years, he was significantly influenced by the Keswick style Biblical ministry and the grace of Canon Scott.

He was first challenged about the direction his life should take at 'The Belfast Young People's Convention', which was originally an integral part of the Portstewart Convention's youth ministry. His parents also took him to the main Convention at Portstewart, and it was there in 1941 that he wrestled with God about the subjects he should study at Grammar School. God had already placed in his mind the idea that he should become a medical missionary and the subjects taken in Senior Certificate would determine his future life. At the Convention Missionary Meeting that year, Oswald heard Mary Russell, a Nursing Sister at the Qua Iboe Mission's General Hospital in Southern Nigeria, tell the gathering that a doctor was urgently needed. God spoke to him, "get ready and get out!" The choice was made – it had to be the sciences with a view to study medicine. Oswald had been taught and challenged by Keswick teaching through Canon Scott, the Belfast YPC and the Portstewart Convention. 'Portstewart' is not a place where people amass knowledge for the sake of it; but rather it is a place in which Spirit led and service directed decisions are made.

After the retirement of Canon Scott, the Mitchell family joined Glengormely Baptist Church in North Belfas, before identifying with the Mustard Seed Mission Church in Vistula Street, Belfast. The fellowship there was rich and Oswald developed as a public speaker, eventually being given responsibility for ministry on one Sunday each month. During those years he was influenced by J.D. Drysdale of Emmanuel Bible College, Birkenhead, the College which had been founded in 1920 to train missionaries for Holiness Societies such as 'The Oriental Missionary Society'. Drysdale was a Scottish Presbyterian but was dissatisfied with their teaching about sanctification. Becoming involved in the Holiness Movement in the early 1900s, Drysdale initiated Holiness Churches in Uddingston and Blantyre under the Church of the Nazarene. Maynard James, joint founder with Leonard Ravenhill, Jack Ford and Clifford Filer of the Calvary Holiness Church, was a regular preacher at the Mustard Seed Hall. This ministry, while much more extreme than Keswick teaching, was to continue the preparation of Oswald's Christian mind for service.

Oswald studied Medicine at the Queen's University of Belfast, indentified with the Bible Union and graduated in 1949. While at Queen's University, he was mentored by Harold William Rodgers OBE, Professor of Surgery (1947-1973) and the Surgical Advisor to the Qua Iboe Mission. Oswald never felt the urge at that time to practice surgery at home and God spoke to him again through the Convention's ministry in the late 1940's and also through a Bible correspondence course he undertook with the Faith Mission. God had challenged him and now he was preparing himself for his missionary service.

During those years he became acquainted with Mr Harry Brown of the China Inland Mission, whose stirring deliverance from the Communists in 1949 is related in Thompson (1959). Oswald recounts that, until graduation, he had no clear guidance concerning an area in which to serve or the specific Mission to approach. Then, very significantly, word reached him that the Qua Iboe Hospital which he had heard about nine years earlier at Portstewart, was again in urgent need of a doctor. Application was made to the Mission and there followed the privilege of serving with that Mission, in two of its hospitals for 15 years.

Reflecting upon those years Mr Mitchell commented:

> During the years of preparation, I was able to attend a number of the Portstewart Convention meetings. These visits proved to be vital, both in deepening my daily devotion and dedication to the Lord, and in forming part of the essential preparation for Christian service, both during the years of training and subsequently in Nigeria and since.

Whilst working at the Royal Victoria Hospital, Belfast, Oswald met a Nursing Sister, Evelyn McCandless. She was a Methodist and it soon became clear that God had brought them together in His will and time. Evelyn was a keen Christian seeking for God's will and eventually the both of them applied to the Qua Iboe Mission. Having been accepted, a Valedictory Service was held in Shankill Road Methodist Church, Belfast and they sailed to Nigeria in 1950 where they were married in December, moving into a mud house built earlier by Bill Holley.

While in Nigeria, they worked quite near a former Qua Iboe Medical Missionary from Belfast. Dr Charles Ross (1903-1964), who served at the Etinan Hospital at Ekpene, Obom and Port Harcourt, and who became "the world's leading leprologist", worked firstly with the Dublin Medical Mission (1926-1928) and then with Qua Iboe until 1947. Dr Ross spearheaded innovative leprosy treatment and medication. He worked in Nigeria, Sierra Leone and Ceylon with national governments and with the World Health Organization. The 1964 British Medical Journal records his work in the form of an Obituary. That work in 1961, according to the Journal, included the care of 300,000 leprosy patients. Dr Ross's father, the Rev. John Ross of Ravenhill

Presbyterian Church was a member of the original Convention Committee and Charles himself was a regular attendee at Portstewart and spoke at the Missionary Meeting in 1933.

From 1950 – 1964, the Mitchells worked with great energy among the people, serving in the Etinan Hospital in the southern Ibeo tribal area and at the Annagn Hospital in the central Annang tribal area. The people were mostly subsistence farmers. As well as their work in the hospitals, Oswald was engaged in film strip evangelism in local villages where they encountered a considerable amount of occultism. Witch doctors were plentiful and Oswald relates an incident of a demon possessed young woman who was tenderly cared for by Evelyn. After much prayer and love this woman was exorcised by the power of Christ.

The Mitchells worked closely with the United Evangelical Church in the North and with the Qua Iboe Church in Southern Nigeria. When the two churches united in 1983, Oswald was delighted to be invited to the ceremony with the Rev. Bill Leach, the Qua Iboe Mission Secretary. The vision of its founder, Samuel Bill, of a Church which was was self-supporting, self-governing and self-propagating, had been realised. Oswald oversaw the building of a Chapel at Etinan Hospital and worked very closely with Sister Marie Cairns, a native of Belfast and member of Ravenhill Presbyterian Church, who gave almost 30 years of service in Nigeria.

Between 1950 and 1964 the Mitchells came home on furlough three times. During these furloughs Oswald completed his Fellowship at the Royal College of Surgeons in Dublin in 1958 and in Edinburgh in 1961, and both Evelyn and he spoke at the North of Ireland Keswick Missionary meetings. God blessed them with two children, and the children remained in Nigeria until they were five years of age. In 1958 and 1961 the children, Ian and Cynthia respectively, returned to Ireland for educational reasons.

In 1964 the Mitchells took the traumatic decision to leave Nigeria. They left behind them a thriving hospital and new converts, many of whom were leaders in the local and national Church in Qua Iboe. Their professional work was not yet completed, for upon returning to N. Ireland, Oswald worked as Senior Registrar at the Belfast City Hospital as an Acting Surgical Consultant for six months and then in the North Down and Ulster Hospitals until 1991. Eventually he retired in 1996 after working in the Royal Victoria Hospital for one year, at the Ulster for an additional two and then finally with the

Department of Social Services. Because of his expertise and close connection with the Portstewart Convention he was invited to join the Committee on 6th February, 1974. He was appointed Treasurer and a Trustee of the Convention in October, 1986. He is committed to Keswick Teaching and is still a member of the Committee where, as a senior man, he is an excellent mentor and wise counsellor.

Evelyn Mitchell died in 2007 after a life of love and service to her Lord, her husband, her family and to Nigeria. Mr Mitchell's entire life was moulded by Keswick Teaching through his local Church, the Convention and the Mustard Seed Hall and was focused on consecrated service in the power of the living Christ. His specific call to full-time service was heard and received at the Convention and the contribution that he and his wife made to the Nigerian people was immense. Convinced that the Kingdom is best advanced though the local church, he is in 2013, an active member of St. Elizabeth's Parish Church in East Belfast.

## The Rev. J.C. Wright:

Joseph C. Wright was a Missionary in Brazil with the Unevangelised Fields Mission (1926 – 1970) and ended his service as the Irish Secretary for the Mission. He had given his life to Christ when 17 years of age through the ministry of the Rev. Nesbitt, the Assistant Minister in Townsend Street Presbyterian Church, Belfast. After his conversion, he worked in the local Sunday school and in the Northumberland Street Mission Hall.

During the 1920s Irish Troubles and subsequent Partition, he was an Ulster Special Constable and he attended the North of Ireland Keswick Convention in 1924. He relates in his autobiography that he was "the only one of the Northern Police Force to be granted leave of absence" in June of 1924. The Convention Speakers that year were the Revs Alexander Frazer, Charles Inwood, J. Russell Howden, A.E. Richardson and Mr G.F. Whitehead. Interestingly, while travelling to the Convention, J.C. Wright met Mr Kalberer, a man of whom he writes, "I had never seen before, nor have I seen or heard of him since. He went out of my life as quickly as he had bumped into it – but the challenge and vision he left me with remained unshakable". The Convention Archives of 1924 record that Mr Kalberer was making his one and only appearance at the Convention and that he was representing the Worldwide Evangelistic Crusade. From Mr Kalberer, J.C. Wright heard about the Red Indians of Brazil. Wright records that a battle raged in his soul during the Convention. He said "Yes" to God's will and then gave up his post with the Police and eventually studied at the Missionary Training Colony in Upper Norwood, London.

On his application form, to the UFM (8th September 1924), Mr Wright gave the Rev. John Ross of Ravenhill, as one of his referees. Joe Wright gave as part of his reason for wanting to serve with UFM, "I want to share the Gospel with those who have never heard that Christ has died." On the same form, the Rev. Nesbitt is recorded as indicating that Joe Wright was "a bright Christian lad". After many years of service among the Red Indians of Brazil, Joe Wright became the Irish Secretary of UFM in 1953.

Through Joe Wright's life and ministry, his brother Fred was called to Brazil. Fred according to his application form to UFM, (July 14th, 1933) had been converted through a Gospel Mission in 1926. At his call to full-time work he asserted that God said to him, "Go ye into all the world and preach the Gospel" – and "I may not disobey". Fred Wright, together with Fred Roberts and Fred Dawson was to be martyred at the hands of the Kayapo Indians sometime in the second half of 1935 and is immortalized in their posthumous title, "The Three Freds". Fred Wright's last letter was found and is, (cited in Light of Life for Unevangelised Fields, June 1937), "If we have success in reaching the Kayapos we will settle amongst them for a few years. If they kill us, we will be in a better place than this".

A Memorial Service was held in the Caxton Hall, London on 30th June, 1936, at which, Belfast man, the Rev. R.U. Gordon Williamson commented (cited by Harris) about his friend, the late Fred Wright,

> ... in intelligence and perseverance Fred was above average. Later his imagination was fired with the need of Amazonia. The speaker himself could not imagine how these three men met their death, but from what he knew of Fred Wright and had heard of the other two, he was sure they were most courageous to the end.

Fred Wright had written a last Will and Testament on 24th May, 1935, in which he expressed the wish that the items he possessed, belonging to his brother J.C. Wright, should be returned. Then he added, (cited by Harris) "the rest of my kit to those who may DV continue the advance to the Kakapos". Generations of young Christians have been inspired by the life, courage, faith and sacrifice of the Three Freds.

At the 2008 and 2012 Conventions at Portstewart, the Rev. Dr Christopher

Joseph Herbert Wright of the Langham Partnership was a Speaker. He is the son of the Rev. Joseph C. Wright and nephew of Mr Fred Wright. No doubt he was challenged and inspired by his father's faith and by his uncle's sacrifice. Through these lives the Convention continues to make a contribution to the Church all over the world!

## James and Dorrie Gunning:

Another veteran missionary who was called at the Convention was Mr James Gunning. His story is movingly told in Maxwell's book (2008). James was called to Missionary Service at the Convention Missionary Meeting while on his honeymoon in 1944, just days after his marriage to Dorrie on 15th June. He felt the call of God to Brazil, did not tell his wife, but prayed that God would call her too. He did indeed call her, two years and three months later.

According to Hazel Miskimmons, a fellow Acre Gospel Mission worker (1961 – 1994), James and Dorrie did pioneer missionary work in Boco do Acre and in Labrea, towns in N.W. Brazil. The Gunnings were life-time missionaries and addressed the Convention Missionary Meeting in 1961, 1966, 1972, 1984 and 1991. They served for 42 years in Brazil, retired home when James became 65 years of age, but returned and finally left Brazil in 1991. James and Dorrie, after their retirement seldom, if ever, missed the annual Convention at Portstewart The grace of Christ radiated from them and they were a great source of encouragement to the Convention Committee by their faithful attendance at the daily Prayer Meeting. Who can tell how many lives they influenced and introduced to Christ?

## The Rev. and Mrs Willard Kelly:

The Rev. and Mrs Willard Kelly served in Nigeria from 1957 to 1980. Willard heard the call of God at the Portstewart Convention in 1947 through the ministry of Mr A. Lindsay Glegg. After acceptance and preparation at both Belfast Bible School (now Belfast Bible College) and the Reformed Presbyterian Church's Theological Hall, Belfast, he departed for Nigeria. While there, he acted as Principal of the Abak Bible College for three years, as Secretary / Treasurer of the Qua Iboe Church for 10 years and as a Station Missionary for 13 years. In addition, a Leprosy Clinic, caring for 100 patients, was located at his station.

Miss Anne Kernohan, in the meantime, was called by God to Qua Iboe at 'The Worldwide Missionary Convention'. After acceptance, she went to serve in

Nigeria as Sister Tutor and Principal of the Nursing Training Home. In 1963, in the Chapel of Etinan Hospital and by special licence, Willard and Anne were married, after a long courtship. The Civil War caused their departure from Nigeria in 1967 and in 1970 they were the first Qua Iboe Missionaries to return. For the next 10 years, Anne taught English and Willard taught theology in the Bible College.

Interestingly, Willard tells about meetings held for the deepening of Spiritual Life in Nigeria. Unlike the early Keswick Movement "no particular theology of Sanctification was taught". However, the call to consecrated living in the power of the Holy Spirit was presented. The Rev. J. Glyn Owen, Minister of Berry Street Presbyterian Church, Belfast was given the opportunity by the Mission's Council to preach at the meetings which were very well attended. The Rev. Owen had preached at Keswick in 1959 and 1965 and at Portstewart in 1961, 1964, 1966, 1968, 1972 and 1979.

When Mr and Mrs Willard Kelly returned to Ireland, Willard was ordained and installed as the Assistant Minister in Knock Presbyterian Church, Belfast in 1983. He was then installed, as Minister in Clogher and Glenhoy in 1984, where both Anne and he served faithfully until retirement in 1995. The Rev. Willard Kelly's call to service was first heard at the Convention and his wife writes about how much she "appreciated the teaching given at the Convention in the years since".

The Convention, by its Missionary emphasis and its teaching of the Bible in the power of the Holy Spirit, has been a tool in the hands of God. The founders of Portstewart had this very goal in mind!

# Chapter 14

# Youth Ministry at the Convention

The founders of the Convention were concerned to make its impact as wide as possible through local Conventions and the Belfast Young People's Convention. Ministry for young people was first suggested by the Committee as early as 1919 when the Minute of 4th July records suggestions being made regarding addressees on special subjects, and meetings for young people. In addition, on 31st March, 1922, it was noted in the Convention Minutes that there were a great number of young converts in the country and that, if possible, a hint should be given to the Speakers to take into consideration the fact, many of them were attending the Convention. It was also suggested that the addresses should be of a very practical nature. The Convention Committee on 31st August, 1923, discussed the possibility of assisting young people who felt called to full-time Christian work at home or overseas.

The first mention of regular Youth Meetings at the Convention was in 1928, as the Minute of 4th April shows, when it was planned that the Rev. Earnshaw Smith, Rector of All Soul's, Langham Place, London would conduct two suitable meetings – one on Wednesday and the other on Friday at 5:00pm. The Convention in 1928 was 14 years old and had been very busy establishing itself in the Northern Irish Church calendar, developing ministry to ministers, acquiring property and planning local Conventions etc.. The Committee was clearly concerned that young people should understand the

Keswick Teaching of full salvation and consecration. Almost every year until 1990 there was a major youth component at the Convention.

In 1929 the speaker at the youth meetings was Mr W.G. Ovens. He was an accomplished and experience youth and children's worker. Ovens spent his early life in Peckham Rye, London and received his formal education at Sidney Sussex College, Cambridge and his theological education at Wycliffe Hall, Oxford. He graduated MA and LLB and was ordained "as a deacon in the Established Church". A thoughtful and passionate evangelical, he wrote the first verse of a well-known hymn,

> Wounded for me, wounded for me,
> There on the cross He was wounded for me;
> Gone my transgressions, and now I am free,
> All because Jesus was wounded for me.

After serving for many years as a volunteer, he sold his share in the family business and began to work full-time for CSSM (Children's Special Service Mission). Later and for some years, he was responsible for the CSSM at Portrush, three miles from Portstewart. Ovens recalled his full salvation experience at Keswick, "these people have got something and I want it". At the 1929 Portstewart Convention, W.G. Ovens gave the closing Friday address on the Work of the Holy Spirit. Although Ovens was invited to conduct the Youth Meetings in 1930, it was decided later that "these meetings will be at 9:00pm next year; the ordinary Convention Speakers should be invited to address them in turn". The Youth Ministry was gradually taking shape and the Convention Committee decided on 15th April, 1930, that the meetings should be held from Tuesday to Friday, with Friday having a missionary flavour.

The Convention's Youth Ministry developed in an ad hoc manner until 1934 when Mr A. Lindsay Glegg was invited to lead it. The meetings were to be held every evening and Mr Glegg "was to have entire charge". His involvement created considerable momentum and in 1934 and 1935 a second tent was erected to accommodate the young people. Around this time the Convention Committee were planning the Belfast Young People's Convention and, according to the Minutes, were also considering ministry to students "perhaps at the University".

In 1936 the Rev. Canon O. Scott reported that the 200 seater tent, belonging to 'The Irish Evangelistic Society', was too small and that a 400 seater would be required for the Youth Ministry. However, the additional cost of hiring the larger tent and the necessary site works to level the ground caused some hesitation. Mr Glegg's business interests meant that he could not always be present for the whole Convention and in 1938 the Rev. Samuel Baxter and others were invited to lead the Youth Meetings. The possibility of extending the Youth Meetings to include Saturday night was considered. In 1941 the largest youth attendance was recorded with the meetings being held in the Presbyterian Church Hall.

The Youth Ministry had become an accepted part of the Convention's life in 1941 and the Convention Committee considered that it needed to be more structured. As a result, a "permanent subcommittee" composed of the Revs J. Dunlop (Convener), J.T. Carson, A.M. Parke, W.G.M. Martin and W.J. Gransden was formed "to take full charge of all the arrangements in connection with the Young People's Meetings". A change in the subcommittee was necessitated by J. Dunlop's appointment as Chairman of Committee in 1944, and the Rev. J.T. Carson was appointed in his place. The Youth Ministry in 1949 and into the mid 1950s seemed to struggle. Mr Glegg was not always present and because various people were leading the events there was a serious lack of continuity from year to year. In 1949 the Rev. A.M. Parke was responsible and in 1955 Tom Rees led the meetings.

Unbelievably from this distance, the Convention Committee on 7th March, 1958, because Mr Glegg was not free to come to Portstewart, decided "in an attempt to lead the young people to concentrate on the main Convention meetings, they [the Youth Meetings] be discontinued for the present year". During the same meeting, the Committee "questioned the continued value of these meetings". At the 1958 Convention it was noted that "there had not been much comment about the discontinuance of the Young People's Meetings". Again in 1959 no Youth Meetings were held. The continuity had been broken and, although the Youth Meetings were led in 1960 by the Rev. J.T. Carson and in 1961 by the Rev. A.W. Rainsbury (Croydon), they were confined to Tuesday, Wednesday, Thursday and maybe Friday if required.

According to the Minute of 11th April, 1963, a renewed effort was made to capture young people. One thousand bookmarks highlighting the meetings were distributed to local School Scripture Union Groups and in 1964, the Rev. Philip Hacking was tasked with the Youth Ministry. During that particular Convention, Mr Hacking expressed the idea that a Youth Meeting on Friday would be purposeful. At the same meeting of Committee and with renewed vigour for Youth Ministry, the Committee decided to adopt the practice of using Friday evening in addition to the other evenings, if the Speaker could stay until the second Saturday of the Convention.

In 1967, the Committee received a letter suggesting that a children's meeting might be held at the Convention under the direction of 'CSSM' or 'Child Evangelism Fellowship'. This was a good idea and was taken up some years later, in conjunction with Scripture Union. However, too few children attended and it was discontinued in 1997. It was taken up again in 2005 and the Convention in 2013, continues to work with the Portstewart CSSM, with both programmes dovetailing. The CSSM workers are commissioned at the Sunday Convention Meeting. One of the Speakers gives a talk to the workers at their base and the Convention advertises the ministry of the CSSM. This is a very successful ministry and, in theory, enables more parents to attend the Convention Meetings.

In the mid 1970s, the Convention Youth Ministry was effectively replaced by Meeting Point. However, according to the Minute of 11th February 1983, "discussion followed on whether some activity specifically aimed at young people should be revived and a subcommittee ... was appointed to consider this matter". In 1983, two Committee members, (Mr N. Lynas and the Rev. H. A. Dunlop) visited Keswick, Cumbria to examine their youth work. Subsequently, they both talked to local youth leaders around the Portstewart area. The Convention Committee considered that whatever Youth Ministry was carried on, it should blend with the main Convention programme and initiate young people into the Convention as such. The decision was made on 5th December, 1984, to hire a small marquee for the Youth Ministry. Dick Dowsett of OMF (Scotland) was invited to be the Speaker. Several house parties were arranged, with the Convention Committee generously underwriting costs for accommodation. Leaflets were inserted into Missionary magazines and the meetings in 1985 and 1986 were a great success. The Rev. H.A. Dunlop reported that 200 young people were resident in house parties and that 500 attended the Saturday evening Youth Meeting, the average age being "late teens and early twenties". This marked a high watermark in attendance. The Youth Ministry drew substantial numbers in 1985 and 1986. The Rev. H.A. Dunlop reported on 21st October, 1986, a general commendation of the "form and content of the programme".

However, the Convention Committee was concerned, if in fact the Youth Meetings "were integrating young people into the main Convention" and it was acknowledged that this "was a long-term objective". The Convention Youth Ministry in 1986 was strong and was making a contribution into many young lives providing Bible teaching in a setting on contemporary worship. Interestingly in 1987, the Youth Meetings adopted three Keswick themes – Failure, Freedom and Fulness. Mr Norman Lynas who had succeeded the Rev. Dunlop as Convener reported, according to the Minute of 25th January 1989,

> while the programme in recent years had attracted a reasonable amount of interest it had not built up a core of support or noticeably increased the interest of younger people in the Convention itself.
> ... It was thought that a move to weeknight meetings following the main Convention gatherings would make the young people's meetings a more integral part of the Convention.

The challenge of making the main Convention Meetings more universally acceptable was debated. If this could be achieved, it was asked, was there any need for a separate Youth Ministry? The local scene changed with the advent of the New Horizon Conference. The effect of its formation was to attract many young people from the Portstewart Convention. Its praise style was more contemporary and although both gatherings eventually had the same type of Speaker, New Horizon became 'the place to be' for young people.

During the 1990s the Convention Youth Ministry was gradually taken over by the Holiday Weekend, held during the closing Friday, Saturday and Sunday of the Convention week. However, on 15th September, 1997, according to the Minutes, the decision was made to close the Convention on Friday evening and not on Sunday. The Youth Ministry then was reduced to a series of Interactive Bible Studies led by the Rev. Martin McNeely and, for example, the Rev. Dr Alec Motyer in 2001. At the 2012 Convention a successful Youth event with 250 people in attendance was held on one evening. Andy Lamberton and his band from Fahan, Co. Donegal provided the music and Nate Morgan Locke from All Souls, Langham Place, London brought relevant teaching from the Bible. The Convention Committee in 2013, is committed to youth ministry and is constantly seeking ways to integrate it into the Convention programme.

# Chapter 15

# Student Camps

D.F. Coggan, writing about the Magee University College, Londonderry Evangelical Union, reports that it "had been the custom of the Union since its inception [on 19th January 1925] to hold a camp at Portstewart, during the North of Ireland Keswick Convention". Coggan relates that, on most days of the camp, a Speaker would come to address the students. Men of the calibre of Bishop Taylor Smith, Mr Lindsay Glegg, Rev. Alexander Frazer and others were used in this capacity. The Dublin University Women Students' Bible Union arranged house parties to the Keswick Convention in 1925, 1926 and 1928. As Coggan shows throughout his book, *Christ and the Colleges*, Keswick Speakers were in much demand at the University Christian Unions in the 1920s and 1930s and were moulding successive generations of students. For example, the Rev. J. Russell Howden addressed the very first meeting of the Queen's University of Belfast's Bible Union. As a result of this definitive connection, Keswick spirituality dominated British evangelical life for decades.

The Rev. John Maddock related his experiences from his personal diary of the Magee Evangelical Union Student Camp in 1949. The camp was a spiritual and recreational retreat for about 36 undergraduates, many of whom were preparing for the Ministry of the Presbyterian Church in Ireland. The six female students resided in a Boarding House while the males stayed in the Presbyterian Church Hall. The camp was self funding and the men had their food cooked by a Mrs McMullan in the local Orange Hall. Mr Maddock's diary indicates that as many as 60 students would have congregated for supper in the evening. The camp was a time for prayer, Bible teaching, swimming and walking in the pleasant seaside area. He recalls prayer times into the small hours of the morning and held in a corner of the tent after the congregation had gone. The students also attended the Youth Meetings. Various Committee members and Speakers came to the Camp to give talks. In addition to the Convention Meetings, some of the students helped at the Open Air Meeting held at the harbour and others assisted with stewarding at the main Meetings. Mr Maddock, although now 83 years of age, attends the Convention every year and his personal spiritual life and ministry was shaped by the experiences he had at the camps many years ago.

Mrs W.J. Lamont commented upon the fact that, in her student days at Magee University College, she attended the student camp along with a number of her female friends. They stayed in a guest house that had been taken over for the Convention by the Egypt General Mission.

The Rev. Malcolm Hare, Minister Emeritus of St. Kentingern's Church of Scotland Parish in Kilmarnock related his experience at the Magee EU Student Camp. He attended from 1946 -1950 and was overcome by his first visit. The Rev. William Still of Aberdeen was the preacher at the opening Sunday evening Meeting in 1947, and his text was John 3:16. During his exposition he took the congregation into the throne room of heaven and listened into the debate in eternity among the members of the Trinity about the sin of mankind and the hope of Salvation. The result being, of course, that the Son became the Redeemer. It all had a profound effect upon Mr Hare. He was ordained in the Church of Scotland in 1956 and served in Gharingcross, Grangemouth, at Langside Hill, Glasgow and at St. Kentingern's from 1979. In 1970 he was invited to preach at the Keswick Convention and in 1975 to speak at the Keswick Holiday Week. Mr Hare remembers the Rev. Geoffrey King giving inspiring talks to the Camp members in 1949.

The Very Rev. Dr Howard Cromie, Minister Emeritus of Railway Street Presbyterian Church, Lisburn, N. Ireland explained that his first visit to the North of Ireland Keswick had been in 1947. He was then a student for the Ministry studying at Magee University College, Londonderry. While there, he worshipped regularly in Ebrington Presbyterian Church when the Rev. W.M. Craig was the Minister. Mr Craig influenced many students to attend the Convention. The Youth Meetings that year impacted him greatly. The large number of young people and the depth of teaching impressed him. The Rev. William Still was a Speaker and he also addressed the student camp. Dr Cromie relates how Mr Still warned the students to be careful about stressing the importance of believers knowing the day and date of their conversion.

Mr Still explained that he did not remember a time in his life when he did not believe in Christ. Coming from a Presbyterian and Reformed position of the Covenant with its stress on paedo baptism, Mr Still impressed Howard Cromie. He also remembers the fun component of the Camp with students not only from Magee but also from the Queen's University of Belfast. The food was served in the local Orange Hall, which just happens to be called the Cromie Memorial Hall! The other thing that impressed him was the Keswick slogan 'All One in Christ Jesus'. This struck him as a wonderful reality that Christians from various Church traditions, who maybe normally would have little contact with each other, could come to the Convention in unity and sit under God's Word. Dr Cromie attended the Convention regularly throughout the 1950s and he believes that the teaching he received there gave him direction for his Ministry and a desire for evangelism. He also attended the Mayallon Camps at the home of Mr R.H. S. Richardson where he received more Keswick style Ministry and shared in the local Quaker Worship Services. At Moyallan he met other men who were to become leaders in the Church. Among them was Jack Shearer, an Anglican who was to become the Dean of Belfast (1985-2001). At the 1951 Portstewart Convention, Dr Cromie relates that the Rev. Harding Wood, a Speaker, talking about worship, said that Divine worship was offered three times each day in his kitchen as he washed the dishes. The young Howard Cromie was impressed by the humanity of holiness. One evening that same year, he drove the Rev. G.R. Harding Wood from the tent to the Speakers' House. Before they parted, Mr Wood laid his hands on Howard Cromie's head and prayed that God would bless his ministry. That simple event is still fresh in Dr Cromie's experience in 2013.

In 1954, he was ordained and installed to the pastoral oversight of Enniskillen Presbyterian Church. In 1955 he attended the Convention, staying in one of the Minister's Houses. The Rev. W.M. and Mrs Craig were the leaders of the House. In 1962 Dr Cromie was called to Railway Street, Lisburn. He was appointed Moderator of the General Assembly in 1984 and was awarded the honorary degree of Doctor of Divinity by the Presbyterian Theological Faculty, Ireland. He became the General Assembly's Convener of the Irish Mission Committee from 1970 – 1978 and of the Church Extension Committee from 1978 – 1982. Both of these posts he filled with evangelistic desire. The Very Rev. Dr Howard Cromie is representative of many, now in full-time Ministry, whose lives were shaped at the Portstewart Convention and who made a significant contribution to the Church throughout the country.

The author this book was an undergraduate at Magee University and Theological Colleges and Trinity College, Dublin, between 1963 and 1967. The EU camps had stopped, but he and several fellow undergraduates took caravans and houses to attend the Convention. Speakers such as the Rev. James Philip of Holyrood Abbey, Edinburgh and the Rev. R.C. Lucas of St Helen's, Bishopsgate, London, came to talk to the men over tea.

The camps were highlighted by the Convention Committee on 1st November, 1973 as a model to attract students back to the Convention. In 1974, Mr Gavin Pantridge, the local UCCF worker, indicated that he was keen to get some undergraduates to attend the Convention and suggested that the Convention could hire a number of caravans for their accommodation. Letters were sent to the various Irish University Christian Unions. In 1974, nine students formed a small house party. In 2013 there is no specific ministry to students although many attend and the 2010-2011 Missionary Project was 'The International Fellowship of Evangelical Students'.

*The Rev. Dr Raymond Brown at the 2000 Convention.*

*The Rev. Dr J.A. Motyer at the 2001 Convention.*

*The Rev. Mark Ashton and his wife Fiona (St Andrew the Great Church of England, Cambridge) at the Castle Erin House Party during the 2002 Convention.*

*The Very Rev. Dean Robert Key, Revs Liam Goligher and Philip Haire at the 2004 Convention.*

*Three Convention Chairmen: Mr Lawson McDonald (1991-2004); Rev. Joseph Fell (2004ff) and the Very Rev. Dr W.M. Craig (1976-1991).*

*Speakers at the 2007 Convention: Revs Liam Goligher, Peter Lewis and Stafford Carson.*

*Rev. Canon R.J. Johnstone and Rev. Johnston Lambe Secretary (2004-2007) and Joint Secretary(2012ff)*

*House Party at Castle Erin, Portrush 2006. Front row from left: Revs David Johnston, J Fell and Dr Charles Price*

*Revs Dr Christopher J.H. Wright and John Woodside at the 2008 Convention.*

*Lunchtime Seminar at 2009 Convention with Revs Noel Agnew, Dr Bob Flayhart and Alastair Morrice.*

*The Congregation praising God during the 2010 Convention.*

*The Belfast City Mission Team in 2011.*

*The Very Rev. Dr W.M. Craig and Mr Oswald Mitchell FRCS – former Chairman and former Treasurer at the 2011 Convention. These two Convention senior statesmen continue to serve as Committee Members and Trustees.*

*All ages enjoy lunch at the 2012 Convention Cafe.*

*From left: Mr Robin Fairbairn (Secretary), Revs Dr Christopher J.H. Wright, Steve Brady, David Scott and Dr Joseph Fell at Rock House during the 2012 Convention.*

*Dedication of the CSSM Team at the 2012 Convention.*

121

# Chapter 16

# Ministry to Ministers

K eswick is not a Church but, by its distinctive ministry, it seeks to encourage local congregations and to stimulate Biblical ministry by empowering ministers. The latter goal was reached through the radical provision of boarding houses for Ministers (1917ff), some of whom were paid for by, what was called, the 'Substitutes Fund' (1925ff); a traditional Breakfast (1920ff) and a Ministers' Meeting (1931ff). It is recorded frequently in the official records that the Very Rev. Dr Henry Montgomery and Mr R.G. Bass were responsible for raising money for the Ministers' House Parties.

In 1917 the decision was taken, on the motion of Canon Scott, to make use of one or two local Boarding Houses for Ministers' House Parties and to seek ways of defraying the expenses involved. The point of the house parties was "to secure the attendance of Ministers who are not in touch with the convention". As this was a new departure for the Convention, it was decided at the same meeting of the Committee to seek advice from the both the Keswick Convention and Bridge of Allan Convention in Scotland. This ministry was to be continued unbroken, and as an integral part of the Convention until 1956. It provided generations of ministers the opportunity of attending the Convention in fellowship with colleagues and, without doubt, it moulded many of them for their ministries. The house parties always had a host and usually a hostess. The Rev. W. and Mrs McCoach hosted the first house party in 1919 when the possibility of a second house was discussed. The local Portstewart Committee in 1921, under guidance from Miss Moncrieff, indicated that some Portstewart friends would keep ministers as guests for the duration of the Convention

The Rev. W. and Mrs McCoach acted as host and hostess until 1927, when Mr

McCoach became unwell and the Rev. S.J. and Mrs Greer acted in their place. In 1928, two houses were taken with the second one being for ministers, who could pay their own way. The Rev. Dr James Little MP and Mr Willis were to invite the ministers as "paying guests" to fill the second house. During the 1928 Convention the possibility of using more than two houses was discussed and in 1930 three were in use. It was agreed to use three houses again during the 1931 Convention. This was the height of the numbers in the Ministers' House Parties and the hosts were the Mr and Mrs Willis, the Rev. S. J. and Mrs Greer, and the Rev. T. and Mrs Rodgers. In 1933, when the fund was in deficit, Mr R. Clyde paid to clear the account. The house party policy was bearing fruit and according to the Minutes of 25th June, 1936, 19 ministers were paid guests in two houses and nearly 100 ministers were in regular attendance at the Convention. According to *The Belfast News Letter* of 25th June 1936, 140 Ministers attended the Breakfast which was held in the then new Town Hall at Portstewart In 1937 the Minutes record the number of attending Ministers as being larger than ever.

A sub committee was formed to select ministers who would be guests of the Convention and from 1939 they assumed the task of generating the necessary funding. From 1942, the Revs S.J. Greer and T. McDermott were responsible for the two houses and in 1943, 27 ministers occupied them. After some internal debate in 1946 about the desirability of having Ministers who were new to the Convention invited, the Minutes record that the houses were filled with mostly new men. The Committee was always careful to ensure that a fair denominational spread was achieved.

In 1951 the Rev. W.M. and Mrs Craig acted as host and hostess. In 1953 the Committee was unsure that the houses were still fulfilling their original purpose and the Committee decided on 31st February, 1956, to discontinue the Ministers' House Parties. During the decades, they had fulfilled a useful and significant role and no doubt the influence of the Convention's Ministry was extended to many Congregations.

As early as 1914, the Convention Minutes record that the need of a Meeting for Ministers was acknowledged. The Revs J. Russell Howden and Dr Alexander Smellie spoke at the very first Ministers' Meeting held in the Cromie Institute, Portstewart on Thursday, 24th June, 1915. The Ministers' Meeting took the form of a Ministers' Breakfast from 1920 until 1952. Mr Clyde and Major McLaughlin hosted the event on the Thursday morning of

Convention week. After the death of Major McLaughlin, Mr Clyde provided the Ministers' Breakfast until he died in 1950. Dr Montgomery is reported in *The Belfast Telegraph* of 25th June, 1936, indicating that Mr Clyde was "one of the most generous men God had ever made". After he died, Mr Richardson and Mrs Clyde assumed responsibility for the breakfast. The Ministers' Breakfast at a Convention ended in 1952.

In 1959 the need for a specific gathering   for Ministers was again acknowledged. Should it be a Breakfast with a Speaker or a Meeting with a Speaker? The first of these Ministers' Meetings with coffee etc. was held on Thursday 23rd June, 1960, at 10:00am with the Rev. Canon Herbert W. Cragg as the Speaker and with the ladies of Portstewart Presbyterian Church serving coffee. The Ministers' Meeting continued in this format until the morning Bible Reading was changed to 11:00am, thus allowing lunch to be served to the ministers.  In 1996, the Rev. Mark Ashton of St. Andrew the Great, Parish Church in Cambridge gave the address. Twenty-five copies were requested and 96 Ministers were in attendance. In 1998 the Rev. David Temple, who for many years had recorded the main Convention messages, began to tape the Address at the Ministers' Meeting.

A change of day occurred in 2001 so that the first Weekend Speaker could stay until Tuesday and address the Ministers' Meeting. Gradually numbers of active ministers attending declined and the number of retired men grew. This was probably due to the influence of other conferences which were attracting younger ministers and the perception that the Portstewart Convention had become jaded. It also reflected the fact that the retired men who were familiar with the Convention and had benefited from its ministry continued to come, whereas the Convention had failed to attract significant numbers of younger ministers.  For younger ministers it was not 'the place to be'! A revamp was attempted with a time of open discussion, notified questions and a buffet lunch. To widen its base, it was decided to include missionaries and other church workers. It was noted that in 2003 more active Ministers were attending the Convention. However, after the 2004 Convention the Committee decided that the Ministers' Meeting should be discontinued as its usefulness had come to an end.

The Rev. Norman Brown, Minister Emeritus of Wellington Presbyterian Church, Ballymena made the following comment in April, 2012.

I first attended Portstewart Convention in 1975 and Rev. Eric

Alexander was teaching at the Bible Readings from the Sermon on the Mount. I had never heard expository preaching before and was astonished to discover that everything he had to say was based on the passage from which he was preaching. His sermon notes were right there in the Bible! The Lord stirred me through this type of preaching and moved me to change the way I handled the Scriptures in my preaching. When I returned to my congregation and started to preach this 'new' way one of my perceptive elders asked, "What happened to you at Portstewart? Your preaching is completely different and so much better!"

This personal testimony is the desired effect of the Convention's ministry to Ministers; that they will love the Lord and His Word and have confidence to preach it in the power of the Holy Spirit so that people feel its impact and God is honoured.

# Chapter 17

# The Belfast City Mission Connection

'The Belfast Town Mission' was established in December, 1827, by the Rev. Reuben John Bryce, a local educationalist and principal of the Belfast Academy, together with "a number of lay and clerical members of the community deeply interested in the spiritual welfare of the non-church going class". All the accounts of the Mission reveal that it was a well organised and efficient body working to the glory of God through many critical periods in the life of the fast growing and rapidly industrialising city of Belfast.

The Belfast City Mission Minute of 27th October, 1851, records that, out of a population of 100,000 people only 15,000 were regular church goers and while £750,000 was spent on alcohol the annual budget of the Mission was only £750. The Mission, from its origin, worked among both the Roman Catholic and Protestant communities. The first Agent to be appointed by the Mission was Mr William Cochrane, a "handloom weaver from Lisburn" and "it is questionable whether any minister in Belfast was the means of more conversions than this Agent of the Belfast Town Mission". In 1888, when Belfast received its City status, the Mission's name was changed to 'The Belfast City Mission'. It had originally been a joint Presbyterian / Anglican enterprise but it came under Presbyterian control, although not officially connected to the General Assembly. The Gospel Missions conducted in the city by Moody and Sankey in the 1870's and by Moody and McNeill in 1892 impacted the city, but it was Torrey and Alexander's Mission in 1903 that made "a considerable impact on the City not least on the districts where the

126

Agents of the City Mission carried on their work".

The Rev. Henry Montgomery, the first Convention Committee Chairman, who was described "as one of the most beloved Ministers in the City", was called into the ministry of the Presbyterian Church through the Moody Mission in 1874. While at the Queen's College, Belfast, he became involved with the Belfast City Mission Hall at McClure Street. Henry Montgomery acted as Honorary Secretary of the Belfast City Mission from 1896 until 1943. He once described the City Mission "as a national asset".

Other leading Christian men in the city acted on the Committees of both the Convention and the City Mission, namely, Mr S.D. Bell and Mr R. Clyde from 1920, the Rev. Wm. McCoach from 1924, and the Rev. J. Dunlop from 1935. Yet another connection with the Convention was the fact that in 1927, at the Mission's Centenary, the Rev. Alexander Frazer, a frequent Portstewart Speaker, was the preacher. In addition Mr T.H. Jemphrey, a Convention Committee member from 1941, was appointed to the City Mission Governing Body in 1947, serving as Honorary Secretary in 1952 and President from 1961 until 1965.

Mr David Hamilton, Secretary of the Belfast City Mission (1960 – 1983), was invited to join the Convention Committee in 1966 and a new era of cooperation began. For many years, the tent had been erected by local fishermen and others, under the direction of several overseers; while stewarding, seating and general tentage during the Convention had been overseen by Mr R.G. Bass, some evangelists from 'The Irish Evangelisation Society', and a number of students. However with the demise of the Society, the Convention Committee had depended upon students alone for help with seating and stewarding. In 1967, David Hamilton, expressed the possibility of providing a number of Belfast City men to assist with these duties. Interestingly, and as early as 1944, an approach had been made to the Belfast City Mission by Mr R. G. Bass for some assistance to augment his team of IES men. The arrangement made with Mr Hamilton was confirmed by the Convention Committee in 1968 and four City Mission men were permitted by the Mission to assist at the Convention. Thus began the even closer and more intimate connection that still pertains in 2013.

Gradually the responsibility for the site during the Convention, for overseeing the erection of the tent by various contractors, which was often contentious, was devolved to the City Mission Team. Seating the tent and the general supervision of it was also devolved to the personnel of the Belfast City Mission. The Rev. Johnston Lambe, a former Secretary of the Mission and of the Convention, explains that this arrangement was never formalised by the City Mission, but it was the accepted practice of the Mission and every Secretary since has facilitated its implementation.

Mr Hamilton continued as Mission Secretary until 1983, and was followed by Mr W. H. Cooke (1983-1991) who had joined the Convention Committee in 1977. Mr Hamilton had been assisted at the Convention by Mr John Luke, the Mission's Assistant Secretary (1972-1974). The ad hoc arrangement took a further turn when Mr Hamilton resigned from the Convention Committee in 1984, with the possibility of Mr Johnston Lambe, replacing him. Mr Lambe, at the time, was the leader of the City Mission team at the Convention and he joined the Convention Committee in 1988.

Johnston Lambe was appointed Secretary of the Belfast City Mission on 1st November, 1990, and continued in office until 1993 when he resigned to take up studies for the Presbyterian Ministry at the University of Ulster and at Union Theological College, Belfast. He was ordained to the Christian Ministry in 1997. The Rev. Lambe was appointed Convention Secretary in 2004 and served until 2007, when he was succeeded by Mr Robin Fairbairn. In 2012, he was appointed as Minute Secretary.

A former City Missionary, the late Rev. Dr J.C. Buick MBE, was largely responsible for the Convention Open Air Meeting in the 1980s-1990s. He was assisted by men from the City Mission, until 1993, when the meeting was discontinued. Dr Buick was Honorary Secretary to the City Mission Committee from 1998, but was not a member of the Convention Committee. Jackson Buick was awarded the MBE by Her Majesty the Queen in 2002 for services to the community as Chaplain in HM Prison, Crumlin Road in Belfast and the Hydebank Young Offenders' Centre during the N. Ireland Troubles. The Presbyterian Theological Faculty, Ireland conferred the honorary degree of Doctor of Divinity upon him in 2004.

The present North of Ireland Keswick Convention Secretary, Mr Robin Fairbairn was appointed in 2007. He had been Assistant Secretary of the Belfast City Mission from 1991 until his resignation in 2003. Under Mr Fairbairn's leadership and expertise the Convention's publicity has been greatly improved. He is responsible for the website and for promoting the Convention. Mr Fairbairn is the Communications Officer of the Presbyterian

Board of Mission in Ireland. His expertise and his many contacts in the media world have been very effective as the Convention has developed in recent years.

There is no doubt about the fruitfulness of the Connection between the two organisations. It was of mutual benefit, for the Missionaries received teaching and inspiration, the Mission was publicized and the Convention was greatly assisted. Mr Bobbi Brown, the current City Mission Secretary, continues the tradition in 2013.

# Chapter 18

# Important Developments (1946-2013)

T he Convention, in its immediate postwar heyday, drew large crowds and was very much 'the place to be' both for younger and older Christians. The Rev. W.P. Nicholson preached at the closing meeting of the 1946 Convention. *The Belfast News Letter* of 26th June, 1946, reported that "a dozen eloquent clergymen attending the Convention" shared their personal testimonies at the Open Air Meeting held at the harbour. Although the local Conventions did not restart after the war, the Convention itself was having a significant spiritual impact on the Church in Northern Ireland and further afield.

From 1946 – 1970 the Convention passed through a period of consolidation following decades of growth from 1914. *The Belfast Telegraph* of 19th June, 1950, reported that 1,500 people were present at the opening meeting and 2,500 at the Sunday evening gathering. However, the soil in which the Convention was living was changing. During the 1960s the Charismatic Movement; then in the 1970s - 1980s the House Church Movement followed by Post Evangelicalism in the 1990s and the Emergent Church Movement of the 2000s, all challenged the Convention. In addition, the rapid marginalisation of the Church and the continuing 'Troubles' affected the spiritual climate in N. Ireland. 1971-1990 were years of transition at Portstewart and were followed by a decade of uncertainty. A gradual transformation was under way and from 2000 the Convention found a new confidence and ever since has experienced renewed growth and vitality.

## Car Park:

In 1959 the Portstewart Rural District Council offered a piece of land, adjacent to the tent site, to the Convention Committee for an agreed price of £125. They bought it! After some years of use as a roughly surfaced car park and further negotiations, the Convention Committee made an agreement with the local Council. They would make the area good for a Public Car Park and the Convention would have its use exclusively during the Convention Week each year. This in effect makes the Convention very accessible. However, with the change of dates into July, many holiday makers who do not attend the Convention make use of the facility and this has presented the leadership with a challenge. The Convention Committee receive £13,000 per year as rent from the Roads Division of the Department of the Environment and this is of great help to the Committee in their budgeting for the Convention.

## Meeting Point:

The late Rev. Dr Alan Flavelle, Minister of Finaghy Presbyterian Church, Belfast was charged by the Convention Committee to plan and host 'Meeting Point'. It was held each year from 1975 till 1982. 'Meeting Point' met in the Presbyterian Church Hall and, on occasions, in the Town Hall after the main Convention Meeting on two evenings. It was an informal gathering at which Dr Flavelle interviewed Speakers and Convention Leaders about relevant subjects. A free cup of coffee or tea was served. 'Meeting Point' generated interest and helped to foster fellowship among Convention attendees. Sadly and for various reasons it came to an end in 1982.

## Crèche:

At the 1975 Convention, the Very Rev. Dr J.T. Carson brought the idea of a crèche to be held during the morning Bible Reading to the attention of the Convention Committee. In 1976 the crèche, meeting in the Presbyterian Church Hall, provided a useful service and allowed parents to attend. The rota was organised firstly by Mrs Joseph Thompson, then by Mrs Sheila Fell and from 1983 by Mrs Linda Lynas. It lapsed for a number of years but now, in 2013, the crèche is a Parent Monitored facility with Closed Circuit Television relayed to the room in which it is held.

## Praise:

The Portstewart Convention was, for years, on the leading edge of innovation as far as praise was concerned. The Keswick Hymnbook, containing much

Keswick hymnody, was used in the worship of God from the very beginning. The Rev. Canon O. W. Scott led the praise for many years and after his death the Revs James Dunlop and Canon W.J. Cooke became responsible for this ministry. The Revs Canon C.J. McLeod and J.T. Carson were added to the team in 1938. Psalms, hymns and choruses were employed. Discussion about using a grand piano took place on 1945. For a number of years a particular hymn was selected for more frequent use. For example at a time of political crisis and spiritual blessing in 1921, a 'Revival Hymn' was printed for distribution to the Convention. The first verse and chorus were;

> There's a sound upon the waters,
> There's a murmur in the air,
> For a move of coming glory fills my soul:
> There's a sigh of a Revival –
> All ye saints prepare for war
> For the hosts of God are marching to the goal.

> Hallelujah! Hallelujah! Hallelujah! To the Lord,
> We shall triumph, We shall triumph
> Through the Everlasting Word;
> There's a sound upon the waters,
> There's a murmur in the air,
> For a move of coming glory fills my soul:

In 1925, Mrs Bessie Porter Head's "Unto the half of my Kingdom" was the "Special hymn sung at the Convention". Mrs Head, from Belfast, was the wife of Mr A.A. Head, Chairman of Keswick and Acting Chairman of Portstewart in 1915 and 1916. In 1918, Canon Scott agreed to bring some friends to form a singing group.

It is well-known that in the 1960s – 1980s there was something of a flood of new praise songs. During those years, the perception was growing that Portstewart was becoming staid. It is a fact that perception matters! There is no evidence, however, that the worship style at the Convention was ever discussed at length until 1984, when the use of more modern and 'scriptural' praise was suggested by the Rev. H.A. Dunlop. An orchestra was first used in 1993 at the both weekends. The Keswick Council discontinued their use of hymn books in favour of TV monitors in 1995 and 'Power Point' was tried at Portstewart in 1996 but due to the translucent nature of the tent roof, was unsuccessful. Throughout the 1990s the Committee sought to develop a contemporary setting of praise for the Convention's ministry.

The Rev. Norman Brown, in conjunction with the Rev. David Temple, undertook to include suitable praise items in the Convention handbook. The Rev. N. Agnew, Sandra Little, James Todd and Philip Kerr, with the help of instrumentalists and the 'Exodus Band', led the praise over a number of years.

Throughout the decades, Mrs Henderson, Mr H.A. Johnston, Mrs Smith, Mr John Henderson and Mrs Marie Millar played the piano at the Convention. Mrs Alison Orr has been the musician at the Bible Readings since 2001. Mr Gary McDowell led the musical group at the evening Meetings from 2005-2009, when the Convention Committee desired to further develop the praise. Mr McDowell played a pivotal role at this stage. Mrs Mildred Rainey was asked to form an orchestra and singing group in 2010 and she continues to do so in 2013 with spiritual sensitivity and great enthusiasm.

Chapter 19

# Prayer and Evangelism at the Convention

As has been noted in this book already, the postwar years were to bring many challenges and changes to the Convention and its leadership team. One constant reality during those years was the Convention's ministry of prayer.

This entire ministry was bathed in prayer both before each Convention and during the Convention week. The Convention has attracted the favour of God. Each day begins with the Prayer Meeting and this has been the practice since the first Convention. At the first Convention Prayer Meeting, the Rev. Evan Hopkins, according to *The Christian* of 2nd July, 1914, took Hosea 14 as his text and from it "gave a clear helpful address". In 1957 the Convention Records indicate that 150 people attended the daily Prayer Meeting. Today the smaller attendance reflects the general decline in congregational prayer meetings. The ministry at the Prayer Meeting was brought by Speakers and Committee members until 2010, when the Convention Committee decided that it should be the responsibility of Committee members only.

The Committee planned to have a weekly Prayer Meeting for the Convention during the months of May and June in 1918 at the Belfast YMCA. The meetings were addressed by some of its members:

| | |
|---|---|
| May 2nd  Rev. Henry Montgomery | May 30th  Rev. James Little |
| May 9th  Rev. F.W.W. Warren | June 8th  Mr S.G. Montgomery |
| May 16th  Rev. Oswald Scott | June 13th  Rev. William McCoach |
| May 23rd  Mr Arthur Pim | June 20th  Mr R.H. Stephens Richardson |

Prayer was a natural reality and practice for the Convention Committee. In 1921, when a financial appeal was being sent out to supporters, the Minutes record, "The members then engaged in prayer for this object and for blessing on the next convention". The practice of the pre Convention prayer times continued, and arrangements were made for them to be held in the Belfast YMCA on the Thursdays in May 1923. When the pre Convention prayer times are mentioned again in the Minutes, it is in 1931 when "it was arranged to hold two special meetings for prayer on behalf of the Convention on Tuesday 9th and 16th June. Throughout the 1930's prayer was often on the Committee Agenda and in 1936 the pre Convention prayer times were standardized as "the usual two Prayer Meetings".

In 1935, an attempt was made to form a 'Portstewart Fellowship' to encourage regular prayer for the Convention. Its inaugural meeting was held in Belfast on 10th April with the Rev. Graham Scroggie as the Speaker.

In 1947, the Committee was told that Mr Lindsay Glegg "had inaugurated a fellowship for those attending the young people's meetings at the Convention which was given the name the League of the Morning Watch". This was a programme encouraging the discipline of 15 minutes prayer and Bible reading each day. There is no record of the League's later development. In addition, the creation of a 'Portstewart Fellowship' with a regular Newsletter to encourage wider interest and prayer was tried again, when Mr R. Clyde introduced the idea in 1948. In 1991 the Committee was told about a Convention prayer group in Portstewart led by the Rev. C.A.B. Williams. Mr W. McDonald also led a local prayer gathering for the Convention in Portstewart for many years. Under the title 'Friends of Portstewart', it was tried yet again in 1993 and 1998 by Mr W.J. Cairns. Sadly, it never really was a numerical success.

In 1944, it was decided to hold an annual 'Day of Prayer' for the Convention Committee and the practice has been continued until 2013. For many years it was held at the home of Mr and Mrs R.H. Stephen Richardson, then in May Street Presbyterian Church Hall, Bible House, Belfast and at the home of Mr and Mrs Burrows at Cultra, Do. Down. Since 1978 the 'Day of Prayer' has met in various Church Halls and Hotels. Occasionally a Speaker at the forthcoming Convention was invited to bring the ministry. In 2012 the Committee decided to locate the 'Day of Prayer' at Portstewart in future.

Originally the Convention was held from Monday to Friday, but because the tent was already erected and seated, it became the practice that the first and second Sunday evenings were given variously to preparation for the Convention and to evangelism. The Convention Committee invited the Rev. W.P. Nicholson to conduct two evangelistic meetings on the first Sunday of the Convention in 1925. They also gave Nicholson the use of the Convention seats for his People's Palace Mission. *The Belfast News Letter* of 29th June, 1946, reported that W.P. Nicholson "will preach at the closing meeting " of the Convention.

The Convention, like Keswick, had a definite evangelistic ministry to its home town from the early 1920s until 1993. The Open Air Meeting at the harbour was under the care of various Committee members, and in 1927 a platform and Keswick motto was provided and the decision was taken to close the meeting at 10:30pm. The Revs McLean, Gibson, Baxter, O'Connor, Mann and McDermott were among those who organised the Open Air into the 1950s. Large numbers attended, many testimonies and short evangelistic talks were given by Speakers. The Rev. W.M. Craig took over in 1952 and it was his responsibility into the 1970s. In 1952, the Committee received complaints from local residents about the interference the public address system was causing. For a short time the Very Rev. Dr John Girvan was in charge. In 1976 the Open Air was held on the first Sunday afternoon, and on Monday, Tuesday and Friday evenings.

The creation of 'Meeting Point' impinged upon the Open Air and in 1983 it was being held on Tuesday and Thursday evenings only. In 1991 it was decided to move it to Sunday afternoon at the Band Stand beside the newly created promenade steps, and to use the Evangelical Youth Movement's drama team.

Open Air ministry throughout the country was in decline in the 1980s. The secularisation of the community reduced the tolerance given to this type of work. The Committee decided with great sadness in 1993 that this evangelistic outreach should be discontinued. Of course, it should be added that all true Bible ministry reaches into the soul and who knows how many people were converted at main Convention meetings?

# Chapter 20

# The Convention in 2013

G od is not only the Lord of the past; He is also Lord of the present and the future. Any church or parachurch group will only minister with relevance if the Reformation principle, 'ecclesia semper reformanda' is applied. God's work is always in need of Biblical reformation so that it is geared to the times and yet remains anchored to the Rock. Constant reformation can be painful, but it is necessary if the Convention is to be an effective tool in an ever changing world. The distinctive spirituality of Keswick is desperately needed in today's church.

In September 2012, the Convention Committee set up structures to ensure that there is good thinking and planning as it faces the future. Several subcommittees, involving all Committee members, have been established. The Convention Trustees are, as always, responsible for the Convention's ethos, its specific direction and the appointment of the Committee office bearers and members. In addition, we are working in conjunction with the Department of Industry, Trade and Investment and with five other large Christian events in N. Ireland: 'New Horizon', 'The Worldwide Missionary Convention', 'Mandate', 'The Faith Mission Convention' and 'Focus Fest'. The Stormont Government Minister is keen to promote these Christian events on the world stage as realities to be experienced.

Among the challenges facing Keswick at Portstewart in 2013 are:

1. To maintain a high level of Bible exposition. That is, faithful exegesis of the Scriptural text with relevant application.

2. To set the Convention in a contemporary worship setting

while remaining faithful to Keswick's distinctive spirituality.

3. To keep the challenge of service at home and overseas before the attendees as an outcome of the priority of consecration to Christ.

4. To work as a complementary agency to the local church by encouraging ministers and other church leaders.

5. To ensure the Convention is kept before the Christian community by the use of attractive and informative publicity.

6. To be inter-generational.

7. To be true to its historic ecumenical roots and to be able to accommodate denominational differences.

The Committee has always wished to engender friendship and fellowship at the Convention. As early as 1926, the Convention Committee decided to provide a "place for lunch for those travelling by motor or charabanc". Since the mid 1990s, they had been providing free refreshments at the daily Prayer Meeting and at various times during the week. In 2009 a café, organised by 'Bon Appétit', was opened and an integrated tent extension was erected to house both the café and the bookshop. The result is that attendees can come for the whole day to the Convention and enjoy both the ministry and the fellowship.

The provision of a good bookshop for the sale of helpful literature has been a priority for the Convention Committee since 1914. Various bodies have been invited to provide the facility, among them Erskine Mayne (from 1914); Scripture Union (from 1971); Mr Dennison of the Bible Society (from 1987); the Faith Mission (from 1996) and '10of those.com' (from 2011) under the leadership of Jonathan Carswell. Originally the book stall was for the sale of Keswick literature and Hymnbooks. After the death of Mrs R.H.S. Richardson in 1938, a Memorial Book Room was generously donated by her husband.

The Committee want to ensure, as far as they can, that Keswick at Portstewart constantly develops its structures, environment and ministry. In 2013 they plan to install plasma screens to assist with the praise and with the flow of information.

# Chapter 21

# Conclusion

Few genuine Christian disciples disagree with Dr Packer's seven principles about holiness:

1. The nature of holiness is transformation through consecration.
2. The context of holiness is justification through Jesus Christ.
3. The root of holiness is co-crucifixion and co-resurrection with Jesus Christ.
4. The agent of holiness is the Holy Spirit.
5. The experience of holiness is one of conflict.
6. The rule of holiness is God's revealed Law.
7. The heart of holiness is the Spirit of love.

The call to holiness is inseparable from our salvation in Christ. Originally, Keswick may have had a question over point five. However, 'Keswick at Portstewart' faces its next century, in the will of God, with a determination to continue honouring and serving Him, proclaiming His Holy Word and calling attendees to consecration and service. The Rev. James Philip of Holyrood Abbey Church, Edinburgh, a frequent and much respected Speaker at Portstewart, saw holiness in terms of 'humanity'. He wrote (cited by J.I. Packer):

> The deepest word that can be spoken about sanctification is that it is a progress towards true humanity. Salvation is essentially considered, the restoration of humanity to men. That is why the slightly inhuman, not to say unnatural, streak in some forms and expressions of sanctification is so far removed from the true work of Grace in the soul. The greatest saints of God have been characterized, not by haloes and an atmosphere of distant unapproachability, but by their humanity. They have been intensely human and lovable people with a twinkle in their eyes.

In 1913, the Rev. Canon Oswald Scott and Mr R.H. Stephens Richardson were fired with the desire to bring Keswick to the North of Ireland. Countless people can say, "Thank God they did". None who ever attended the Convention with a sincere desire for God went away disappointed, because the leaders surrounded the faithful Speakers of the Word with prayer and they trusted the Holy Spirit for the outcome.

May all who read this book continue to work out their own "Salvation with fear and trembling, for it is God who works in you to will and to act according to His good purposes" (Philippians 2:12b-13). Thank God because "He who began a good work in you will carry it on to completion until the Day of Christ Jesus" (Philippians 1:6b).

*Gloria in excelsis Deo!*

# Select Bibliography

Barabas, S. 1952. So Great Salvation. London: Marshall, Morgan & Scott.

Bebbington, D.W. 1989. Evangelicalism in Modern Britain – A History from the 1730's to the 1980s. London and New York: Routledge.

Boardman, W.E. 1859. The Higher Christian Life. Edinburgh: Alexander Strahan and Co.

Brown, P.E. 2012. Ernest Kevan, Leader in Twentieth Century British Evangelicalism. Edinburgh: The Banner of Truth Trust.

Carson, J.T. 1963. Ocean Fulness. Belfast: The Portstewart Convention Committee.

Carson, J.T. 1966. Alexander Frazer of Tain. Glasgow: United Committee of Christian Organisations.

Carson, J.T. 1988. The River of God is Full. Belfast: The Portstewart Convention Committee.

Chapman, A.G. 2001. Moyallon Camp Fellowship – a Record of God's Grace 1934-2001.Lurgan: Home Mission Committee of Ulster Quarterly Meeting of the Religious Society of Friends in Ireland.

Chapman, A.G. 2005. 100 years and more: history of Friends in Portadown, 1655-2005. Lurgan: Lurgan Friends Meeting.

Collins, P. 1994. Irish labour and Politics in the Late Nineteenth and Early Twentieth Centuries. (*In* Collins, P. *ed.* Nationalism and Unionism – Conflict in Ireland 1885-1921. Belfast, Institute of Irish Studies: The Queen's University of Belfast. p.123-145)

Coggan, F.D. 1934. Christ and the Colleges. London: Inter Varsity Fellowship of Evangelical Unions.

Cooney, DL 2006. Sharing the Word. A History of the Bible Society in Ireland. Blackrock: Columba Press.

Corbett, J.S. 1991. Bill Holley, more than a Doctor. Belfast: The Qua Iboe Fellowship.

Corbett, J.S. 1965. Joseph Ekandem – Chosen Vessel, Faithful Steward. Belfast: Qua Iboe Publication.

Corbett, J.S. 1977. According to plan: the story of Samuel Alexander Bill, Founder of the Qua Iboe Mission, Nigeria. Worthing: Walter.

Edwards, D. 1984. Christian England – from the 18th Century to the First World War. London: Collins.

Fell, J. 2013. The Portstewart Convention Connection. (*In* Bailie, P. *ed*. Unity, Faith, Peace and Progress in Qua Iboe Mission and Mission Africa. Belfast: Mission Africa. (In press).

Figgis, J.B. 1914. Keswick from Within. London: Marshall Bros.

Fitch, T. 1980. The Very Rev. James Dunlop MA, DD, Oldpark Presbyterian Church, Belfast, N. Ireland. Belfast: Hallidays.

Fulton, A.A. 1970. Biography of J. Ernest Davey. Belfast: Presbyterian Church in Ireland.

Gordon S.D. 1904. Quiet talks about Prayer. New York: Pyramid.

Gordon, S.D. 1906. Quiet talks about Jesus. 2nd ed. London: Hodder & Stoughton.

Gordon S.D. 1912. Quiet talks about Our Lord's Return. Fleming H. Revell originally 1912. Reprinted by OCR 2009.

Harris, L.F. 1961(?). Our Days in His Hands: A Short History of the Unevangelised Fields Mission. London: Unevangelised Fields Mission.

Hartford-Battersby, T.D. & Moule, .C.G. 1890. Memoir of T.D. Harford-Battersby London: Seeley and Co., Ltd

Harford, C.F., ed. The Keswick Convention, its Message, its Method and its Men. London: Marshall Brothers. (141-155).

Houghton, F. 1953. Amy Carmichael of Dohnavur. London: SPCK.

Hyson-Smith, K. 1989. Evangelicals in the Church of England 1734 – 1984. Edinburgh: T & T. Clark.

Johnston, E.H. 1901. The Highest Life – A Story of Shortcomings and a Goal including a Friendly Analysis of the Keswick Movement. New York: A.C. Armstrong & Son.

Kevan, E.F. 1953. The Saving Work of the Holy Spirit. London: Pickering and Inglis

MacMahon, B. 1994. The Story of Ballyheigue Castle. Thaidhg: Oideacht.

Marshall, W. 1692 [1981]. Gospel Mystery of Sanctification. Hertford: Evangelical Press.

Maxwell, V. 2008. Lives lived unto Him. Belfast: Acre International.

McKeown, R.L. 1902. In the land of Rivers, the Story of the Qua Iboe Mission. London: Marshall Bros.

McKeown, R.L. 1912. Twenty Five Years in Qua Iboe – the Story of Missionary Effort in Nigeria. London: Morgan and Scott.

McKeown, R.L. 1935. My Tour in Qua Iboe. Belfast: Qua Iboe Mission.

Megaw, J. et al. 2004. The Sun-Dailled Meeting- Houses, Cullybackey. Cullybackey, Ballymena: The Congregational Committee, Cunningham Memorial Presbyterian Church.

Murray, I.H. 2010. Evangelical Holiness. Edinburgh: Banner of Truth. www.banneroftruth.co.uk

Orr. J.E. 1965. The Light to the Nations. Exeter and Plymouth: Paternoster.

Packer, J. I. 1955. "Keswick" and the Reformed Doctrine of Sanctification. The Evangelical Quarterly. 27 (3):153-167

Packer, J. I. 1984. Keep in Step with the Spirit. Leicester: Inter Varsity Press.

Packer, J. I. 1992. A passion for Holiness. Leicester: Crossway Books.

Packer, J.I. 2009. Rediscovering Holiness. Ventura, CA: Regal

Peirson, A. T. 1897(?). The Story of Keswick and its Beginnings. London: Marshall Bros.

Plum R.H. 1945 (?). Bessbrook – A record of industry in a Northern Ireland Village Community and of a Social experiment 1845 – 1945. Belfast: The Bessbrook Spinning Company Ltd and J.N. Richardson, Sons and Owden.

Pollock, J.C. 1964. The Keswick Story. London: Hodder and Stoughton.

Price, C. & Randall, I.M. 2000. Transforming Keswick. Carlisle: Paternoster.

Redpath, A. 1967. Deliverance from Sin. (In. Stevenson H.F. ed. Keswick Week. London: Marshall, Morgan and Scott. p. 85-89).

Rowlandson, M. 1997. Life at the Keswick Convention – a personal recollection. Cumbria: OM Publishing.

Russell, E.A. 1983. A History of Oldpark Congregation – a twentieth century Belfast Church over eighty years. Belfast.

Ryle, J.C. 1879. Holiness. Darlington: E.P. Books.

Scotland, N. 2009. Apostles of the Spirit and Fire: American Revivalists and Victorian Britain. Milton Keynes: Paternoster.

Scott, O.W. 1934. The Story of Portstewart Convention 1914 – 1934. Belfast.

Sibbett, R.M. 1926. For Christ and Crown- The Belfast City Mission. Belfast: The Witness Office.

Sloan, W.B. 1935. These Sixty Years. London: Pickering and Inglis.

Smiles, Samuel. 1859. Self Help: the art of achievement illustrated by accounts of the lives of great men. Sphere and originally published by Murray in 1859.

Stott, J.R.W. 1966. Men made New. Leicester: Intervarsity Press.

Thompson, P. 1959. The second Watch – a biography of Mr Harry Brown of Belfast. London: China Inland Mission.

Warfield, B.B. 1931. Perfectionism. Philadelphia: The Presbyterian and Reformed Publishing Company.

Wright, J. C. 1975. Living to the Will of God. Belfast: Published privately.

# Annexure

## Missionary Meetings 1914 – 1997

*Sources: Convention Archives and Minutes*

*This annexure records numbers of Missionaries attending and the Missionaries who participated at the Missionary Meeting.*

1914 – Missionaries attending not recorded

| | |
|---|---|
| Rev. J. Omelvena | Irish Presbyterian Foreign Mission |
| Mrs Bill | Qua Iboe Mission |
| Mr George Swan | Egypt General Mission |

Source for 1914 -*The Christian*, (1914:2nd July)

1915 – Missionaries attending not recorded

No details

1917 – Missionaries attending not recorded

Presbyterian Zenanna Mission

Qua Iboe Mission

Church Missionary Society

1918 – Missionaries attending not recorded

No details

1919 – Missionaries attending not recorded

No details

1920 – Missionaries attending not recorded

No details

1921 – Missionaries attending not recorded

No details

1922 – Missionaries attending not recorded

Every Missionary present is to address the Missionary Meeting

Capt. Gracey       Armenia

1923 – Every Missionary present is to address the Missionary Meeting

1924 – From 13 attending Missionaries

No details

1925 – 19 attending Missionaries
No details
1926 – 25 attending Missionaries
No details
1927 - 21 attending Missionaries
No details
1928 - 29 attending Missionaries
No details

1929 – Missionaries attending not recorded

| | |
|---|---|
| Miss K. Channing | Egypt General Mission |
| Miss Warburton Booth | Zenana Bible Medical Mission |
| Mr J. Nelson | Qua Iboe Mission |

*The above 3 to speak at the Friday afternoon Convention Meeting.*
Minutes (1929: 27th June)
*The following spoke at the Saturday Mission Meeting.*

| | |
|---|---|
| Miss Eileen O. James | Christina Mission to the Jews |
| Mr W.H. Robinson | J.T.M. (?) |
| Mrs H.J. Mason | China Inland Mission |
| Mr A. Brown | S.M.M (?) |
| Miss K. O'Hanlon | South America General Mission |
| Rev C.W. Jebb | Church Missionary Society |
| Mr Harrison | World Wide Evangelisation Crusade |
| Rev. J. Perry Horton | Ceylon and India General Mission |

1930 – 8 attending Missionaries
No details

1931 – 12 attending Missionaries
Minutes (1931: 25th June) indicated that almost 50 were present at the (Missionary) tea.

| | |
|---|---|
| B.S. Rosenthal | Church of Ireland Jews Society |
| Goodlet Hamill | Egypt General Mission |
| Wm McComb | Heart of Amazonia Mission |
| Dr Stanley Smith | Ruanda General Medical Mission |

| Miss Lucy McCord | Africa Inland Mission |
| H.W. Dickson | Qua Iboe Mission |
| R.E. Hanna | Jungle Tribes Mission |
| Rev. A. Sills | Church Missionary Society (China) |
| Frank McCarthy | China Inland Mission |

**1932 - Missionaries attending not recorded**
9 Societies represented at Missionary Meeting. Minutes, (1932:30th September)

**1933 – 6 attending Missionaries**
| Mr B.S. Rosenthal | Church of Ireland Jews Society |
| Miss J.H. Ramsey | Zenana Bible and Medical Mission |
| Mr Wm. H. Webb | China Inland Mission |
| Miss E. McGalliard | Egypt General Mission |
| Mr H.G. Farrant | Sudan United Mission |
| Dr C.M. Ross | Qua Iboe Mission |
| Mr J. Savage | Evangelical Union of South America |
| Mr John Purves | Worldwide Evangelisation Crusade |

**1934 – Missionaries attending not recorded**
| Mr B.S. Rosenthal | Church of Ireland Jews Society |
| A.K. Macpherson | China Inland Mission |
| Mrs Dr Stevenson | Irish Presbyterian Mission (India) |
| Mrs E.H. Ward | Egypt General Mission |
| Miss T. M. Skipper | Church Missionary Society (Ruanda) |
| Mr E.H. Smith | Sudan United Mission |
| Mr Donald Currie | Qua Iboe Mission |
| Mr L. Herniman | Evangelical Union of South America |

**1935 - Missionaries attending not recorded**
| Mr B.S. Rosenthal | Church of Ireland Jews Society |
| W.F.H. Briscoe | China Inland Mission |
| Miss N. Rees | Worldwide Evangelisation Crusade |
| Miss S.S. J. Murdock | Egypt General Mission |

| J. Ballentyn | Sudan United Mission |
| C.S. Bebbington | Qua Iboe Mission |
| Wm. McComb | Unevangelised Fields Mission |
| Miss D. Hunter | Irish Presbyterian Mission |
| Pastor J. Harrison | Evangelical Union of South America |

## 1936 – 33 attending Missionaries

| Rt Rev. Dr F.W.S. O'Neill | Irish Presbyterian Mission (Manchuria) |
| Mr H.H. Mercer | Egypt General Mission |
| Miss W. Walker | Church Missionary Society (Ruanda) |
| Miss C. Cheal | Sudan United Mission |
| Mrs I. McEwan | Qua Iboe Mission |
| Mr E. Boyce | South African General Mission |
| Dr A.E. Fraser-Smith | Bible Churchman's Missionary Society |
| Miss J. Cullen | Methodist |
| Rev. E.J. Mann | China Inland Mission |
| Miss A. Perse | Unevangelised Fields Mission |

## 1937 – 30 attending Missionaries

| Mr Herman Newmark | Hebrew Christian Testimony |
| Mr L.J. Lyall | China Inland Mission |
| Miss N. Bennett | Church of England Zenana Missionary Society |
| Mr Wm. Richmond | Sudan United Mission |
| Mr Donald Currie | Qua Iboe Mission |
| Miss C.M. Tucker | Egypt general Mission |
| Mr Alex Jardine | Evangelical Union of South America |

## 1938 – 36 attending Missionaries

| Mr Herman Newmark | Hebrew Christian Testimony |
| Mr R.E. Thompson | China Inland Mission |
| Miss Grills | Irish Presbyterian (China) |
| Mr E.J. Ardill | Egypt General Mission |
| Mrs Richmond | Sudan United Mission |
| Mr D.H. O'Neill | Qua Iboe Mission |
| Dr J. Nairn Hay | Inland South America Mission |

| Mr G.R. Bennett | Irish Baptist Mission (Argentina) |
| Mr J.A. Stewart | Europe |

## 1939 – 28 attending Missionaries

| Miss E. Lessynski | Church of Ireland Jews Society |
| Rev. W.E. Wallner | Barbican Mission to the Jews |
| Mr W.J. Wiseman | British and Foreign Bible Society |
| Miss I.J. S. Murdock | Egypt General Mission |
| Mr G. Gaussen | China Inland Mission |
| Pastor William Usen | Qua Iboe Mission |
| Mr Edgar Bryson | Africa Inland Mission |
| Miss Nancy Williams | Zenana Bible and Medical Mission |
| Rev. W.H. Graham | Jungles Tribes Mission |

## 1940 – 2 attending Missionaries

| Miss E. Lessynski | Church of Ireland Jews Society |
| Rev. Dr Arnold Frank | Irish Presbyterian (Jewish) |
| Rev. James McCammon | Irish Presbyterian (Manchuria) |
| Mr H. H. Mercer | Egypt General Mission |
| Mr I. McEwan | Qua Iboe Mission |
| Rev. J. Darashah | Dipti Mission (India) |
| Mr Stanley Reid | Baptist Mission (Peru) |

## 1941 – 14 attending Missionaries

| Miss E. Lessynski | Church of Ireland Jews Society |
| Miss M. Spearman | Ceylon and India General Mission |
| Mr A. Crockart | Irish Presbyterian (Jungle Tribes) |
| Miss N. Williams | Zenana Bible and Medical Mission |
| Miss R. Forsythe | Church Missionary Society (Tanganyika) |
| Mrs I. McEwan | Qua Iboe Mission |
| Mr H.H. Mercer | Egypt General Mission |
| Miss M.A. Shackelton | China Inland Mission |

## 1942 – 19 attending Missionaries

| Miss E. Lessynski | Church of Ireland Jews Society |

| | |
|---|---|
| Miss K.D. Scott | Hebrew Christian Testimony to Israel |
| Miss I. J. S. Murdock | Egypt General Mission |
| Miss I. Gilliland | Church Missionary Society (Palestine) |
| Rev. W.L. Wheatley | Qua Iboe Mission |
| Miss A. Mitchell | Worldwide Evangelisation Crusade (Belgium Congo) |
| Miss C. Shearborn | Church of England Zenana Mission (India) |
| Mrs S.B. Keers M.D. | Irish Presbyterian (Manchuria) |

1943 – 21 attending Missionaries

| | |
|---|---|
| Miss E. Lessynski | Church of Ireland Jews Society |
| Mr H. H. Mercer | Egypt General Mission |
| Miss Emma Munn | Worldwide Evangelisation Crusade |
| Mrs Tett | Sudan United Mission |
| Mr H.W. Dickson | Qua Iboe Mission |
| Miss H. Stewart | Irish Presbyterian (Manchuria) |
| Miss E.A. Knight | Church of England Zenana Mission (India) |
| Miss M.E. Fleming | Zenana Bible and Medical Mission (India) |
| Rev. H.S. Meadows | Bible Churchman's Missionary Society (Burma) |

1944 – 13 attending Missionaries

| | |
|---|---|
| Miss K.D. Scott | Hebrew Christian Testimony to Israel |
| Mr E.J. Ardill | Egypt General Mission |
| Miss A. Mitchell | Worldwide Evangelisation Crusade |
| Mr C.S. Benington | Qua Iboe Mission |
| Mr J. Mooney | Sudan Interior Mission |
| Miss L. Bottom | Zenana Bible and Medical Mission |
| Mrs Cannell | Church of England Zenana Mission (China) |

1945 – 28 attending Missionaries

| | |
|---|---|
| Miss E. Lessynski | Church of Ireland Jews Society |
| Miss Newman | Egypt General Mission |
| Mrs Milliken | Worldwide Evangelisation Crusade |
| Dr Manwell | Church Missionary Society |
| Miss K. Spence | Sudan Interior Mission |

| | |
|---|---|
| Mr W. Richmond | Sudan United Mission |
| Mr W.E. Dornan | Qua Iboe Mission |
| Dr Stevenson | Irish Presbyterian (India) |
| Mr HM Brown | China Inland Mission |
| Rev. O.F. Peskett | Bible Churchman's Missionary Society |

1946 – No list of names of attending Missionaries recorded

| | |
|---|---|
| Rev. J. Barkey | Hebrew Christian Testimony to Israel |
| Mrs H.N. Bryson | Africa Inland Mission |
| Mr H.W. Dickson | Qua Iboe Mission |
| Mr Goodlett Hamill | Egypt General Mission |
| Rev. R. Iiiff | Church Missionary Society |
| Rev. W.H. Hudspeth | British and Foreign Bible Society |
| Mr R.E. Thompson | China Inland Mission |
| Mrs H.O. Pritchard | Regions Beyond Missionary Union |
| Dr W.B. Johnston | Bible Churchman's Missionary Society |
| Mr W.I. Creighton | Baptist Foreign Mission (Peru) |

1947– No list of names of attending Missionaries recorded

| | |
|---|---|
| Miss Leszynski | Church of Ireland's Jews' Mission |
| Rev. H.E. Jump | Sudan United Mission |
| Mr V.L Carson | Worldwide Evangelisation Crusade |
| Mr Bennington | Qua Iboe Mission |
| Mrs Giesner | Egypt General Mission |
| Rev. Maxwell Orr | China Inland Mission |
| Rev. Wilfred Crittle | Bible Churchman's Missionary Society |
| Mr A. Jardine | Evangelical Union of South America |
| Mr J.C. Wright | Unevangelised Fields Mission |
| Mr C.H. Morris | British and Foreign Bible Society |

1948 – from 30 attending Missionaries

| | |
|---|---|
| Mr Feldman | Hebrew Christian Testimony to Israel |
| Mr C.W. Wylie | Qua Iboe Mission |
| Mr T. Archibald | Sudan Interior Mission |
| Mr N.A. Tucker | Egypt General Mission |
| Mr W.J. Wiseman | British and Foreign Bible Society |

| Miss Lily Boal | Worldwide Evangelisation Crusade |
| Mr E. Wigg | Army Scripture Readers |

## 1949 – from 37 attending Missionaries

| Miss Leszynski | Church of Ireland's Jews' Mission |
| Rev. W.L Wheatley | Qua Iboe Mission |
| Miss Pat Still | Bible Churchman's Missionary Society (Ethiopia) |
| Rev. J.B. Mooney | Sudan Interior Mission |
| Miss Naish | Egypt General Mission |
| Miss E. Couche | Church of England Zenana Medical Mission |
| Mr R. E. Thompson | China Inland Mission |
| Miss Hope Lee | Regions Beyond Missionary Union (India) |
| Mr S. Reid | Irish Baptist Foreign Mission |

## 1950 – from 44 attending Missionaries

| Rev. J. Barkey | Hebrew Christian Testimony to Israel |
| Rev. T.R. graham | Qua Iboe Mission |
| Rev. J. Cardoo | Sudan United Mission |
| Bishop Fred Morris | Bible Churchman's Missionary Society |
| Miss Gillian Lamb | Egypt General Mission |
| Miss L.M. Simonsen | British Syrian Mission |
| Mr A. L. Haig | British and Foreign Bible Society |
| Rev. A.L. Keeble | China Inland Mission |
| Rev. W. McReynolds | Irish Presbyterian Foreign Mission |
| Rev. Robert Martin | Ludhiana Women's Christian Medical Mission |

## 1951 – from 34 attending Missionaries

| Miss Leszynski | Church of Ireland's Jews' Mission |
| Rev. W.H. Graddon | Qua Iboe Mission |
| Miss M. Lloyd | Africa Inland Mission |
| Mrs F. Walker | Egypt General Mission |
| Mr J.C.F. Robertson | British and Foreign Bible Society |
| Miss I. Webster-Smith | Japan Evangelistic Band |

| | |
|---|---|
| Miss K.M. Griggs | Church of England Zenana Missionary Society |
| Miss E.G. Armstrong | Irish Presbyterian Foreign Mission |

1952 – No list of names of attending Missionaries recorded

| | |
|---|---|
| Miss K.D. Scott | Hebrew Christian Testimony to Israel |
| Rev. W.L. Wheatley | Qua Iboe Mission |
| Mr T. Ardill | Sudan Interior Mission |
| Mr Goodlett Hamill | Egypt General Mission |
| Miss V. McGrath | Japan Evangelistic band |
| Mr H.O. Pritchard | Regions beyond Missionary Union |
| Miss Mary Harvey | Acre Gospel Mission |

1953 - No list of names of attending Missionaries recorded

| | |
|---|---|
| Miss Leszynski | Church of Ireland's Jews' Mission |
| Dr B. Holley | Qua Iboe Mission |
| Rev. Canon E.J. Webster | Bible Churchman's Missionary Society |
| Miss E. McGalliard | Egypt General Mission |
| Mr A.W. Marthinson | British and Foreign Bible Society |
| Miss Amy McBurney | Regions beyond Missionary Union |
| Mr Wesley Gould | Unevangelised Fields Mission |

1954 - from 17 attending Missionaries

| | |
|---|---|
| Miss K.D. Scott | Hebrew Christian Testimony to Israel |
| Rev. H.W. Dickson | Qua Iboe Mission |
| Rev. J.B. Mooney | Sudan Interior Mission |
| Mr Alan Tucker | Egypt General Mission |
| Miss D.M. Dove | C.I.M. / Overseas Missionary Fellowship |
| Miss Sarah Paul | Irish Presbyterian Foreign Mission |
| Rev. Canon Chandu Ray | British and Foreign Bible Society |
| Mr A. Jardine | Evangelical Union of South America |

1955 - No list of names of attending Missionaries recorded

| | |
|---|---|
| Miss Harari | Church of Ireland Jews Society |
| Mr Norman Dack | Qua Iboe Mission |
| Miss Gwen Kerr | Bible Churchmen's Missionary Society |

| | |
|---|---|
| Mrs M. Evertsberg | South Africa General Mission |
| Rev. Noel L. White | Church Missionary Society |
| Miss H. Holmes | Egypt General Mission |
| Miss J. McCormick | Japan Evangelistic Band |
| Mr A. Johnston | CIM / Overseas Missionary Fellowship |
| Mr Cecil Courtney | Jungle Tribes Mission (Irish Presbyterian Foreign Mission) |
| Dr Hugh Montgomery | Evangelical Union of South America (Peru) |

## 1956 - from 33 attending Missionaries

| | |
|---|---|
| Miss I. Samson | Hebrew Christian Testimony to Israel |
| Dr W.M. Holley | Qua Iboe Mission |
| Mrs E.L. Liley | North Africa Mission |
| Dr D. Milton-Thompson | Church Missionary Society |
| Mr Bryce H. Gray | China Inland Mission |
| Dr J. Stevenson | Irish Presbyterian Foreign Mission |
| Mr A.S. Robinson | New Testament Missionary Union |
| Rev. W.G. Nelson | Ceylon and India General Mission |

## 1957 - from 26 attending Missionaries

| | |
|---|---|
| Miss K.D. Scott | Hebrew Christian Testimony to Israel |
| Mrs W.H. Holley | Qua Iboe Mission |
| Mrs R. McAllister | Unevangelised Fields Mission |
| Miss Emma Munn | Worldwide Evangelisation Crusade |
| Miss E. McGalliard | Egypt General Mission |
| Rev. S.B Moles | Jungle Tribes Mission |
| Miss Molly Harvey | Acre Gospel Mission |

## 1958 - from 24 attending Missionaries

| | |
|---|---|
| Mr H.J. Clarke | Qua Iboe Mission |
| Miss Mary Coles | South Africa General Mission |
| Mr A.G. King | Middle East General Mission |
| Mr H.O. Prichard | Regions beyond Missionary Union |
| Mr George McCormick | Ceylon and India general Mission |
| Rev. J.H. Davey | Irish Presbyterian Foreign Mission |

| | |
|---|---|
| Miss M.E. Wilkinson | Dohnavur Fellowship |
| Miss Jean Anderson | C.I.M. / Overseas Missionary Fellowship |

1959 - from 36 attending Missionaries

| | |
|---|---|
| Miss I. Leszynski | Church of Ireland Jews' Society |
| Dr W. M. Holley | Qua Iboe Mission |
| Dr S. Lindsay | Africa Inland Mission |
| Miss Joan Nicholson | Ruanda Mission of the C.M.S. |
| Rev. C.S. Benington | Bible Society |
| Mr E.N. Crocker | Worldwide Evangelisation Crusade |
| Dr John Stevenson | Irish Presbyterian Foreign Mission |
| Miss may Campbell | C.I.M. /Overseas Missionary Fellowship |
| Miss Violet McGrath | Japan Evangelistic band |
| Mr Samuel Sloan | Irish Baptist Foreign Mission |

1960 - from 34 attending Missionaries

| | |
|---|---|
| Miss K.D. Scott | Hebrew Christian Testimony to Israel |
| Miss Mary Russell | Qua Iboe Mission |
| Miss Cicely Radley | Egypt General Mission |
| Rev. T.M. Orr | China Inland Mission |
| Rev. W.J. McIlfatrick | Oriental Missionary Society |
| Mr John Warner | Irish Presbyterian Foreign Mission |
| Mr Martin Snow | Unevangelised Fields Mission |

1961 – from 26 attending Missionaries

| | |
|---|---|
| Miss I Samson | Hebrew Christian Testimony to Israel |
| Mrs O. Mitchell | Qua Iboe Mission |
| Mr R. McAllister | Unevangelised Fields Mission |
| Dr Victor Gardiner Bible | Churchman's Missionary Society |
| Miss E. Graham | Bible and Medical Missionary Fellowship |
| Miss Jean McCormick | Japan Evangelistic Band |
| Miss S. Minnis | Soldiers and Gospel Mission |
| Mr J. Gunning | Acre Gospel Mission |

1962 – from 22 attending Missionaries

| | |
|---|---|
| Miss I. Leszynski | Church of Ireland Jews' Society |
| Mr W.G. Johnston | Qua Iboe Mission |
| Dr R.J.D. Anderson | Africa Inland Mission |
| Mr T. Archibald | Sudan Interior Mission |
| Miss E. Mc Galliard | Middle East General Mission |
| Rev. W.G. Nelson | Ceylon and India General Mission |
| Rev. C.G. Eyre | Methodist Missionary Society |

1963 – from 35 attending Missionaries

| | |
|---|---|
| Miss Maureen Skelly | Qua Iboe Mission |
| Miss Rebe Firth | Worldwide Evangelisation Crusade |
| Dr Neville Everard | Bible Churchman's Missionary Society |
| Dr John Breeze | Irish Presbyterian Foreign Mission |
| Mrs H.O. Pritchard Regions | Beyond Missionary Union |
| Mr Edmund Norwood | Unevangelised Fields Mission |
| Mr J. McVicker | Irish Baptist Foreign Mission |

1964 – from 31 attending Missionaries

| | |
|---|---|
| Rev. J. Vieire | European Missionary Fellowship |
| Miss Dorothy Martin | Qua Iboe Mission |
| Mr A. Stewart | Sudan Interior Mission |
| Miss E. Rainey | Africa Inland Mission |
| Miss S. McLaughlin | Bible and Medical Missionary Fellowship |
| Miss P. Flannigan | Dr Graham's Homes |
| Miss M. McComb | Regions Beyond Missionary Union |
| Miss May Campbell | China Inland Mission / OMF |
| Mr Fred Orr | Acre Gospel Mission |

1965 – from 33 attending Missionaries

| | |
|---|---|
| Miss M. Harari | British Jews Society |
| Dr Helen Roseveare | Worldwide Evangelisation Crusade |
| Miss Kathleen Payne | Qua Iboe Mission |
| Miss Pixie Caldwell | Sudan United Mission |
| Miss Beattie Burns | Irish Presbyterian Foreign Mission |

| | |
|---|---|
| Miss Violet McGrath | Japan Evangelistic Band |
| Mr Martin Snow | Acre Gospel Mission |

**1966 - from 33 attending Missionaries**

| | |
|---|---|
| Miss M. Calder | Mission-Foi-Evangile |
| Rev. W.H. Dickson | Qua Iboe Mission |
| Mr N.A. Tucker | Middle East General Mission |
| Rev. W.B. herd | Bible Churchmen's Missionary Society |
| Dr J.S. Davies | Bible and Medical Missionary Fellowship |
| Mr J. Gunning | Acre Gospel Mission |

**1967 - from 33 attending Missionaries**
No Details

**1968 - from 38 attending Missionaries**

| | |
|---|---|
| Miss Huguette Harari | International Jews Society |
| Rev. W.H. Gradden | Qua Iboe Mission |
| Miss Jean Nicholson | Church Missionary Society |
| Mr H. O. Prichard | Regions Beyond Missionary Union |
| Miss J.L. Anderson | Overseas Missionary fellowship |
| Miss Sally Foley | Evangelical Union of South America |

**1969 – from 35 attending Missionaries**

| | |
|---|---|
| Mr E. Kerr | Qua Iboe Mission |
| Miss E. Kisby | Sudan Interior Mission |
| Miss Rebe Firth | Worldwide Evangelisation Crusade |
| Dr James Barton | Irish Presbyterian Foreign Mission |
| Miss Sheila McLaughlin | Bible Medical Missionary Fellowship |
| Miss May Campbell | Overseas Missionary Fellowship |
| Mr John McVicker | Irish Baptist Foreign Mission |

**1970 – from 38 attending Missionaries**

| | |
|---|---|
| Rev. W.H. Graddon | Qua Iboe Mission |
| Miss Gwen Kerr | Bible Churchmen's Missionary Society |
| Rev. Norman Duncan | Oriental Missionary Society |

| Miss V. McGrath | Japan Evangelistic Band |
| Mr Alfred Johnston | Overseas Missionary Fellowship |
| Miss Betty Jones | Unevangelised Fields Mission |
| Miss Sadie Minnis | Gospel Mission of South America |

1971 – from 33 attending Missionaries plus 1 Missionary Child, Gloria Sessoms

| Miss Meta Dunlop | Qua Iboe Mission |
| Mr R.J. Harbinson | Worldwide Evangelisation Crusade |
| Miss Jean Anderson | Overseas Missionary Fellowship |
| Mrs E. Prichard | Regions Beyond Missionary Union |
| Mr Jim Hunter | Bible and Medical Missionary Fellowship |
| Rev. R. Armstrong | Methodist Missionary Society |
| Mr Martin Snow | Mission House of Prayer, Brazil |
| Rev. John Sessoms | Unevangelised Fields Mission |

1972 – from 24 attending Missionaries

| Miss Doreen Adams | Africa Evangelical fellowship |
| Mr Willard Kelly | Qua Iboe Mission |
| Miss Violet McComb | Middle East General Mission |
| Rev. J. Black | Oriental Missionary Society |
| Miss HM Glass | Overseas Missionary fellowship |
| Mr J. Gunning | Acre Gospel Mission |
| Mr V. Cardoo | Christian Literature Crusade |

1973 – from 25 attending Missionaries

| Mr John Ransom | Qua Iboe Mission |
| Rev. John Selfridge | New Life for All |
| Mr David Strachan | Overseas Missionary Fellowship |
| Miss Audrey Weir | Unevangelised Fields Mission |
| Mr H.O. Prichard | Regions Beyond Missionary Union |
| Miss E. McGalliard | Middle East general Mission |

1974 – from 34 attending Missionaries

| Mr R. Thompson | Qua Iboe Mission |

| Rev. Kenneth Todd | Methodist Missionary Society |
| Dr Francis P. Cotterell | Sudan Interior Mission |
| Miss Jean Anderson | Overseas Missionary Fellowship |
| Mr V. Maxwell | Acre Gospel Mission |
| Mr J. Smyth | Oriental Missionary Society |

1975 – from 31 attending Missionaries

| Mr W.J. Kelly | Qua Iboe Mission |
| Mr J. Selfridge | Message of Victory Evangelism - Zambia |
| Mr J. Hunter | Far East Broadcasting Association – India |
| Mrs A. Johnston | Overseas Missionary Fellowship – Philippines |
| Mr Fred. Orr | Acre Gospel Mission - Amazonas |

1976 – from 18 attending Missionaries

| Miss Mary Wilson | Africa Inland Mission |
| Mr N. Alan Tucker | Middle East General Mission |
| Mr Wesley Bell | Worldwide Evangelistic Crusade |
| Miss Margaret McComb | Regions Belong Missionary Union |
| Mr John Sessoms | Unevangelised Fields Mission |

(Mr Sessoms was not present at the Missionary Meeting and Miss May Walker, Regions Beyond Missionary Union, Peru, was asked to take his place).

1977 – from 29 attending Missionaries

The Minutes of 23rd June 1977 do not include the Missionaries selected to speak at the Missionary Meeting.

1979 – from 28 attending Missionaries

| Mr James Simms | Qua Iboe Mission |
| Miss Gwen Kerr | Bible Churchman's Missionary Society |
| Mr Douglas Cowan | Church of Scotland Overseas Mission |
| Mr Samuel Sloan | Irish Baptist Missions |
| Mr Fred Orr | Acre Gospel Mission |

1980 – Missionaries attending not recorded in Archive 1

| Miss Mary Wilson | Africa Inland Mission |

Mr David McConkey                  Bible and Medical Misionary Fellowship
Miss Maud Wilkinson                Overseas Missionary Fellowship
Rev. John Sessoms                  Unevangelised Fields Mission

1981 – Missionaries attending not recorded in Archive 1
Miss Barbara Dyatt                 Bible and Medical Misionary Fellowship
Miss Elsie Quinn                   Overseas Missionary Fellowship
Mr Robert Toner                    Japan Evangelistic Band
Mr Alfred Johnston                 Overseas Missionary Fellowship
Mr Bertie Hamilton                 Regions beyond Missionary Union

1982 – Missionaries attending not recorded in Archive 1
Dr Helen Roseveare                 Worldwide Evangelistic Crusade
Mrs J.C. Simms                     Qua Iboe Mission
Mr Raymond Reeves                  United Mission to Nepal
Miss Jean McCormick                Japan Evangelistic Band
Canon W.R. Kelly                   Bible Churchman's Missionary Society

1983 - No information in Minutes (1983: 23rd June) or Archive 1

1984 – Missionaries attending not recorded in Archive 1
Mr Desmond Hales                   Africa Inland Mission
Miss Pixie Caldwell                Sudan United Mission
Dr Jean Shannon                    Irish Presbyterian Foreign Mission
Mr John Millar                     Overseas Missionary Fellowship
Mr James Gunning                   Acre Gospel Mission

1985 – Missionaries attending not recorded in Archive 1
Dr Esther Davis                    Qua Iboe Mission
Rev. Robin Quinn                   Presbyterian Foreign Mission
Mr Peter Crawford                  International Christian Fellowship
Miss Mildred Andrews               Overseas Missionary Fellowship
Mr Maurice Sloan                   Unevangelised Union of South America

1986 – Missionaries attending not recorded in Archive 1

| | |
|---|---|
| Miss Elsie Quinn | Overseas Missionary Fellowship |
| Mr Robert Toner | Japan Evangelistic Band |
| Miss Mary Alexander | Overseas Missionary Fellowship |
| Miss Sybil Hogg | Evangelical Union of South America |
| Mr Samuel Sloan | Irish Baptist Mission |

1987 – Missionaries attending not recorded in Archive 1.
Minutes (1987: 25th June) states that comment was made on the relatively few serving missionaries attending the Convention this year.

| | |
|---|---|
| Mr James Simms | Qua Iboe Mission |
| Rev. Wilson Gordon | Presbyterian Overseas Board |
| Miss Pauline Galbraith | Operation Mobilization |
| Mr Alfred Johnston | Overseas Missionary Fellowship |

1988– Missionaries attending not recorded in Archive 1.
Minutes (1988: 23rd June) states that again very few serving Missionaries attending the Convention.

| | |
|---|---|
| Mr George McCormick | International Christian Fellowship |
| Miss Margaret McComb | Regions Beyond Missionary Union |
| Miss Elsie Quinn | Overseas Missionary Fellowship |
| Dr Tom Geddis | Acre Gospel Mission |

(Dr Geddis was a former Acre Gospel Mission worker and would soon become the local area Representative for the Mission)

1989 – Missionaries attending not recorded in Archive 1.

| | |
|---|---|
| Miss Violet McComb | Middle East Christian Outreach |
| Miss Anne Roberts | Overseas Missionary Fellowship |
| Mr David Morgan | European Christian Mission |
| Miss Mary Wilson | Africa Inland Mission |
| Mr Sidney Garland | Qua Iboe Mission |

1990 – Missionaries attending not recorded in Archive 2.

| | |
|---|---|
| Mr Tom Lewis | BEE International |
| Pastor Desmond Hales | Africa Inland Mission |
| Miss Mildred Andrews | Overseas Missionary Fellowship |
| Dr Esther Davis | Qua Iboe Fellowship – note new name |

Mr William Hamilton　　　　Oriental Misionary Society

1991 – Missionaries attending not recorded in Archive 2.
Miss Pixie Caldwell　　　　Action Partners
Miss Lynda McFerran　　　　Overseas Missionary Fellowship
Mr James Gunning　　　　　Acre Gospel Mission
Mr John Brew　　　　　　　Irish Baptist Missions.

1992 – Missionaries attending not recorded in Archive 2.
A representative from the following Societies spoke:
Middle East Christian Outreach
Africa Inland Mission
Interserve
Operation Mobilisation

1993 – Missionaries attending not recorded in Archive 2.
Mr Wilson McMahon　　　　Overseas Misionary Fellowship
Miss Sheila McLaughlin　　　Interserve
Miss Mary Steele　　　　　Wycliffe Bible Translators
Miss Esther Kennedy　　　　Sudan Interior Mission
Miss Nancy Gill　　　　　　Oriental Misionary Society

1994 – Missionaries attending not recorded in Archive 2.
Miss Violet McComb　　　　Middle East Christian Outreach
Miss Maizie Smith　　　　　Unevangelised Fields Mission

1996 – Missionaries attending not recorded in Archive 2.
No details

1997 – Missionaries attending not recorded in Archive 2.
No Details.

1998 – No Missionary Meeting held.

*Source: Convention Archives and Minutes*